Anatole G. Mazour

Women in Exile:
Wives of the Decembrists

Women in Exile:
Wives of the Decembrists

Anatole G. Mazour

Professor, Emeritus
Stanford University

THE DIPLOMATIC PRESS

TALLAHASSEE, FLORIDA

Published by

THE DIPLOMATIC PRESS, INC.
1102 Betton Road
Tallahassee, Florida 32303

©1975 The Diplomatic Press, Inc.

Library of Congress Catalog Card No. 74-22111
ISBN 91052-19-1

*A list of other Diplomatic Press publications
appears at the back of this book.*

Printed in the United States of America.

Library of Congress Cataloging in Publication Data

Mazour, Anatole Gregory, 1900 -
    Women in exile : wives of the Decembrists.

    Bibliography: p
    1. Siberia—Exiles. 2. Women in Siberia.
3. Russia—History—Conspiracy of December, 1825.
I. Title.
DK770.M35   322.4'2'0957   74-22111
ISBN 0-910512-19-1

Preface

The year 1975 marks the 150th anniversary of the Decembrist revolt (December 14/26, 1825), which had sought to bring constitutional government to autocratic Russia. The poorly organized exponents of freedom, mostly aristocrats, military officers, and intellectuals, were easily crushed and harshly punished. Much has been written about the abortive plot, little about the tragedies that befell individuals and families in its aftermath, virtually nothing of the wives of the Decembrists. This is the remarkable story of the wives and fiancées of the Decembrists who of their own volition followed their men into exile in Siberia.

While the nation, temporarily stunned and silenced, was left brooding over the hollow dreams of the Decembrists, the wives of the victims accepted realities in a different manner: they chose to share the severe penalties imposed upon their men by a panicky administration. To some compatriots their journey into exile seemed a senseless act of youth, but others viewed it as feminine heroism and loyalty, as a deed of genuine inspiration.

The conduct of the women was the more remarkable when one realizes the atmosphere which prevailed in the country shortly after the Decembrist revolt. There was widespread fear that anyone suspected of "Decembrist thinking" might pay dearly for cherishing dangerous alien ideas. The harsh verdict confirmed the government's fear of being compromised by the testimony extracted from the Decembrists. In view of the situation, the wives' publicly declared readiness to follow their husbands into exile bordered on political defiance. It was this heroism that inspired P. A. Vyazemsky to conclude that the Decembrist wives were bound "to grant history a few beautiful lines."[1]

[1] *Perepiska A. I. Turgeneva s Vyazemskim*, I, 1814-1833, 56.

Pushkin obliquely referred to the events when he wrote in "The Prophet" at this time:

And with his sword my breast he cleft
My quaking heart thereout he reft,
And in the yawning of my breast
A coal of living fire he pressed.

Then in the desert I lay dead,
And God called unto me and said:
'Arise, and let My voice be heard,
Charged with my Will go forth and span
The land and sea, and let my Word
Lay waste with fire the heart of man.'

(Tr. by Maurice Baring)

Most of the women who ventured to the hinterland of the empire — to Irkutsk, Chita, Nerchinsk, Turinsk or Oyek — were of high cultural and social prominence. Cuddled by privilege, pampered by wealth, tenderized by leisure, and made effeminate by education, they miraculously turned into pillars of strength, into symbols of endurance and perseverance. Their decision to join their husbands or, as in the case of two of them, to follow the men they loved and to marry them in exile, could not be swayed either by family members or officials, including the Emperor himself. Marie Volkonskaya did not bow to the threat of her father, the national wa hero General N. N. Rayevsky, that he would disinherit and disown her if she followed her husband into exile. Rayevsky long resented the action of his daughter. At first he did not wish to write to her or even to forward her mail to Siberia. But with time he came to respect her fortitude and her loyalty to her husband. *"C'est la plus admirable femme que j'ai connue,"* he exclaimed on one occasion as he pointed to his daughter's portrait.

Fourteen out of eighteen wives of the Decembrists shared the fate of their husbands. Six of them had to leave behind a total of thirteen children, several of whom died. New children were born in Siberia, but conditions there were so harsh that seven mothers lost an aggregate of twenty-two children.

What is perhaps most striking is that there is not a single clue in the past of any of these women to explain where they acquired that astonishing will, tenacity, or forthrightness which they were to display. Prior to their going to Siberia not one of them had ever belonged to a secret society or shown the slightest political proclivities.[2] Aristocratic in origin, they were preoccupied with family or social life.

As the women set out on their hazardous journeys east in pursuit of their "state criminal" husbands, they had no romantic illusions. They were grimly aware of the privations and physical and mental agonies that lay ahead in the years of exile. The women set out for Siberia, even though it was popularly regarded as the "icebox" of Russia, from which there was no returning. And indeed, by the time the amnesty for which they prayed was granted in 1856, few of them were left alive to rejoice in the event. The extraordinary courage which it must have taken for the women to abandon their comfortable homes and to move to such a land makes their story—to paraphrase Peter Geyl—a historical legend without end.

The author has the pleasure to express his indebtedness to the following persons, who assisted in the publication of this study. To the members of the Hoover Library staff for their never failing cooperation in locating material,

[2] P. Y. Annenkova, *Zapiski zheny dekabrista* (Petrograd, n.d.), 72. Marie N. Volkonskaya, *Zapiski,* 23. See also *Muzey dekabristov* (Moscow, 1923), I, 1-3, 5, where the wife of K. Ryleev might have found out at the last moment of the existence of a clandestine society. Cf. *Russkaya starina,* III, 1901, 673-674.

references or films. To Professor George A. Lensen for his able editorial assistance and helpful suggestions that made this study more readable. To my wife, Josie, for her unfailing cooperation and endurance while this study was in the process of preparation. To all of them my profound gratitude.

September 1974
Stanford University   A.G.M.

Contents

Preface v

1. Background and Decision 1

2. Trubetskaya 13

3. Departure Eastward. 21

4. On to Nerchinsk 35

5. Marie Volkonskaya .57

6. Two French Brides .79

Epilogue 91

Documents 97

Biographical Data 123

Select Bibliography .130

One cannot but be sorry that such eminent, genuine Russian women, representing such a moral force as the wives of the Decembrists, have not been appreciated or found their Plutarch . . . . Models of self-denial and self-sacrifice, of love and extraordinary energy . . . . They are examples the country can be rightly proud of and serve as ideal models for future generations.

Belogolovyi, N. Vospominaniya.
Moscow, 1897.

Our hearts we tear apart, 'tis true
But tell me, Father dear,
What else would'st thou have had me do?
Would grief avail, or fear?
The one who could have helped I trow
Must be . . . . Oh, Father pray
Forgive and bless the daughter now
To cheer her lonely way![1]

[1] Nicholas Nekrasov, *Russian Women*, tr. by Juliet M. Soskice (Oxford University Press, 1929), 3. See also S. Reiser, "Nekrasov o rabote nad 'Russkimi zhenshchinami,'" *Zvenya*, VI, 1936, 701-736.

1

Background and Decision

According to the sentence handed down by the Supreme Criminal Court in June 1826, five of the participants in the uprising of December 1825 were to be hanged; ninety were punished by hard labor imprisonment, followed by banishment into exile for life. The sentences given by the military courts subsequently also included various terms of exile for some of the participants. During the nights of July 21 and 23, 1826, the first parties of the Decembrists began their long trek to Eastern Siberia.

Since no instructions designated the exact locations to which the exiles were to be sent, the governor of Irkutsk temporarily distributed them at various nearby plants, such as the Uralsk salt mines or the Alexandrovsk brewery.[2] But the Third Section of the Imperial Chancellery, which was in control of the political police, considered this as contrary to the wishes of Tsar Nicholas I, who wanted the Decembrists dispatched to the mines of Petrovsk, a suburban area of Nerchinsk. The Decembrists were hastily sent

[2] See S. N. Chernov, "Dekabristy na puti v Blagodatsk," *Katorga i ssylka,* book XVIII, 1925, 246-275.

beyond Lake Baikal and temporarily kept in the Chita region in such places as the Alexandrovsk silver melting plants. Not until September 1830 were they moved to the specially constructed prison at Petrovsky zavod, a suburb of Nerchinsk.

The group of "state criminals," removed from western Russia to the eastern borders of the empire, included not only the most prominent members of the secret organizations formed during the first quarter of the nineteenth century, but the most western oriented, European educated, intellectually enlightened men of their generation. Their exile marked a sorrowful page in the Russian liberal movement of the nineteenth century and a fiasco in the efforts to introduce a constitutional government in the land of absolute autocracy.[3]

Shortly after the men sentenced to imprisonment and exile had departed for Siberia, an entirely different group gathered to follow them. These were the wives and fiancees of the exiles, who set out along the same itinerary, determined to share the fate of their husbands and beloved. Among them were some of the most socially prominent members of Russian society. Their decision became a symbol of feminine loyalty and devotion.

At first officials were at a loss how to cope with the women who had earnestly expressed the desire to follow the state criminals to Siberia. Since they were already (or in the case of the fiancées were about to become) the wives of "criminals," what would be their legal status? Should the government allow them to go to Siberia at all? It was an unprecedented situation that urgently required clarification.

[3] See Anatole G. Mazour, *The First Russian Revolution, 1825* (Stanford University Press, 1967), 220 ff. The first group included Prince S. Trubetskoy, Prince S. Volkonsky, Artamon Muraviev, V. Davydov, the brothers Andrei and Piotr Borisov, and A. Yakubovich.

The historian is in possession of a remarkable document that casts at least a partial light on the subject. It is an order that had been issued by the Governor General, A. S. Lavinsky, to the governor of Irkutsk, I. B. Zeidler. Its nature is of such importance that it deserves to be mentioned.[4]

In a special note Governor General Lavinsky warned the authorities of Irkutsk that in view of the decision of some of the Decembrist wives to follow their men to Siberia, the administration was under the obligation to explain to these women the hazards involved in such an adventure. Lavinsky speculated, and rightly so, that since these women came from most prosperous families, they would carry with them considerable sums of money as well as valuables. This was in itself, Lavinsky thought, a hazard in view of the presence of a considerable criminal element throughout Siberia. It was very likely also, Lavinsky contemplated, that many of the women would be accompanied by serfs.

In view of these factors, Lavinsky advised the Irkutsk administration to act as follows: (a) All serfs who accompanied the women would be freed; (b) upon reaching Irkutsk the women were to be advised once again and for the last time that they ought to return west for their own good. Should they refuse to do so, the administration must warn them of the following: (1) That their status would henceforth be that of "wives of exiled labor convicts," with all the legal, political, and social implications; (2) that the children born in Siberia would be considered as "state peasants" (*possessionnye krestyane*); (3) for reasons of personal safety they must turn in all valuables as well as money in their possession to be kept by the local treasury of Irkutsk.

[4] "Iz proshlogo. K istorii dekabristov," *Istorichesky vestnik*, V, 1898, 675-677; V. Pokrovsky, *Zheny dekabristov*, 2-3.

Despite all the rules issued by the authorities and formally signed by Governor General Lavinsky, the exact legal status of the women when they came to Siberia to join their convicted husbands remained at best uncertain and judicially imprecise. As mates of exiled state criminals the wives were subjected to loss of their civil rights. But for what length of time? While in residence with their husbands only? Did they regain their rights whenever they returned to western Russia? And could they return at all? These questions were never clarified, nor even answered; no public pronouncements were made, no rulings issued by the courts.

The status of the children was equally important. According to the laws of the empire, children of noble parents must be given proper education to enable them in due course to render service to the state appropriate to their class. But as one high official argued—and Nicholas I appears to have agreed with the interpretation—that if the fathers were in exile or in prisons, the children could not avail themselves of the educational facilities; furthermore, their fathers could not serve as models of political or moral conduct.[5]

From the very beginning the idea was to dissuade the women from going to Siberia. If this could not be done, all authority was to be applied to warn them of the gravity of their decision—of the desponded existence they faced in Siberia due to the severe climate and the limitation of judicial rights.

Perhaps the most vexed question was the right of the women to take their children with them.[6] The Decembrist I. D. Yakushkin made his wife promise to him that under

---

[5] The entire question is lucidly discussed by P. E. Shchegolev in his essay, "Zheny dekabristov i vopros ob ikh yuridicheskikh pravakh," *Istoricheskie etiudy* (St. Petersburg, 1913), 395-441.

[6] See *Golos minuvshego*, XI, 1913, 194-195.

no circumstances would she join him in Siberia unless she was granted the right to take their children with her.[7] After lengthy arguments, she was issued the desired permit, but was warned that there were no educational facilities whatever in Siberia to train her boys. As it turned out, one of Yakushkin's sons became ill and was unable to travel at the designated date. Since Mme Yakushkina had promised her husband that she would not leave her children behind, she did not depart as planned when she was ready to proceed to Siberia. The officials ruled that no new permit could be issued, since the original one had been allowed to lapse. Repeated requests by Mme Yakushkina to join her husband were turned down by the government.

The prospect of parting with their children was, of course, at least as anguishing an experience for the mothers as for the fathers. Mme Marie Volkonskaya was absolutely forbidden to take along her one-year old boy. The shock was the greater when she learned shortly after her departure that her only son had died. Mme Trubetskaya was forced to leave her two children, a girl and a boy. Her boy too died after a brief illness. Baroness Rosen and Mme Yushnevskaya were able to join their husbands only after their respective sisters consented to assume responsibility for the care of their offspring. Mme Fonvizina departed after she managed to entrust her two boys to her mother. Mme Davydova, a mother of five, was forced to divide her children among various relatives.

Once the women decided to join their husbands, they virtually severed all relations with home. Even their parents were not allowed to visit them in exile. The prisoners were forbidden to communicate with relatives in western

[7] I. D. Yakushkin, *Zapiski* (St. Petersburg, 1905), 129-130. See also *Russkie propilei* (Moscow, 1915), I, 85 ff.; I. D. Yakushkin, *Zapiski, stati, pis'ma;* Commentary by S. Y. Shtraikh (Moscow, 1951), 95-96.

Russia, though this rule was not always rigidly enforced. On various occasions some of the women managed to receive messages that kept them informed about family life in western Russia and even abroad.

It was understood that once the women obtained official consent to return to western Russia under some special circumstances, the issued permission would be accompanied by a number of restrictions. For example, if a husband died during exile, the widow would be assigned a specific location for residence. Thus, as late as 1844, when the Decembrist A. P. Yushnevsky passed away, his 54-year old widow was not allowed to return west. A year later the Decembrist A. V. Yental'tsev died, barely completing his term of hard labor imprisonment. The court ruled, as in the case of Yushnevskaya, that Mme Yental'-tseva must remain in Siberia, at Yalutorovsk (presently known as Beriozov). Totally exhausted from long years of exile and hardships, Yental'tseva argued that Yaluto-rovsk with its harsh climate, was injurious to her health, but her petition for permission to move elsewhere was disregarded. It was not until the amnesty of 1856, issued by Alexander II shortly after his ascent to the throne, that Mme Yental'tseva was able to return to Moscow, where she died three years later.

Two documents issued by the administration shed light on the judicial rights of the Decembrist wives. One was the above-mentioned order, issued by the Governor of Irkutsk, with the approval of Nicholas I, formulated by Prince Dolgorukov in St. Petersburg. It concerned children of noble birth whose parents had been convicted for one reason or another. The second document was a compilation of decisions passed from time to time concerning the wives of the Decembrists who resided in Siberia.

Thus, on September 19, 1826, the prison commandant was notified that wives of the Decembrists who lived with their husbands were not entitled to any domestic servants. Wives who lived separately were permitted to see their husbands once every two days and could employ two servants, one male and one female. The commandant was instructed to see that neither the Decembrists nor their wives would receive any large sums of money either in cash or in any other form, but only the amount specified by prison regulations. This amount was to be paid through the office of the commandant. The initial sum to set up house was not to exceed 2,000 rubles, followed by an annual allowance of not more than 1,000 rubles. All correspondence must go through the office of the commandant.

A juridical difficulty was created by the fact that two of the women were French citizens. One was Pauline Geueble (later known as Praskovia Yegorovna Annenkova); the other one was Camilla Ledantu (later known as Camilla P. Ivasheva). Their insistence to follow the men they loved and to marry them in Siberia sounds more like the theme for a novel than like history. The case of Mlle Camilla Ledantu was briefly as follows.[8] Mlle Ledantu secretly fell in love with Ivashev and never revealed her emotional state either to Ivashev himself or to anyone else. It was not until 1830, nearly four years after Ivashev had been exiled to Siberia, that she confessed to her mother that she was in love with him, and now sought permission to join him in matrimony.

The other woman, Pauline Geueble, was the daughter of a French colonel killed in Spain by the guerrillas. She appealed to Nicholas I directly to be permitted to follow Annenkov, with whom she was deeply in love, to Siberia. The Emperor endeavored to dissuade her and after some futile efforts to change her mind, in a moment of rare

---

[8] The Decembrist I. D. Yakushkin offered a different theory stripped of all romance. See Yakushkin, *Zapiski, stati, pis'ma dekabrista,* 172-176.

magnanimity, not only consented to let her go, but granted her 3,000 rubles for travel expenses.

The well-known poem of N. A. Nekrasov, "Russian Women," was dedicated to two of the wives, Mme Trubetskaya and Mme Volkonskaya. The poet A. I. Odoevsky also dedicated a deeply stirring poem to Volkonskaya, whom he described as the lady "who was daily waiting at the fence through which her heavenly utterances led drops of honey pass to the prison inmates . . . ." But the other wives deserve similar praise, for all of them shared the heavy burdens of Siberian exile. Nor, as mentioned, were all of them "Russian women." The poetic exaltations, however beautiful, give no real picture of the human tragedy that befell all the persons concerned.

The main question that arises is what were the deeper motivating factors that compelled these women to cast aside their former way of life and to wander off into an unknown land, into the uncertain world of Siberian exile? Some were undoubtedly motivated by marital loyalty and deep love. To these their heroism seemed as natural as acceptance of the luxury they had enjoyed in the past. Such, for instance, must have been the case of Mme Trubetskaya, the first one to accept the challenge fearlessly. In the words of Nekrasov:

> A life of deep and boundless woe
> My husband's fate will be,
> And I do not desire to know
> More happiness than he.[9]

Mme Marie Volkonskaya and Baroness Anna V. Rosen most likely belonged to the same category. But there were other women in this heroic saga, who by nature at least, were less poised and less sophisticated, though

[9] The poem "Russian Women" has been translated into English by Juliet M. Soskice. See N. A. Nekrasov, *Poems* (Oxford University Press, London, 1929).

equally valorous. As an illustration of this type may be cited Elizabeth P. Naryshkina, the restless, lonely woman, who was more contented to be by herself than in any company, always secretive and physically not too well. Others, such as A. V. Yental'tseva, were more sociable, irrepressible, somewhat petulant, but lovable extroverts. They added vivacity to the dull life of the feminine community.

The first woman to venture on the hazardous journey was Yekaterina (Katasha) I. Trubetskaya, quickly joined by Marie N. Volkonskaya. They were followed by E. P. Naryshkina, Alexandra V. Yental'tseva, N. D. Fonvizina, Pauline Gueble (Annenkova), and Camilla P. Ledantu (Ivasheva), to mention only a few. To join their men they had to overcome not only numerous barriers raised by officialdom, but the objections raised by their parents, especially the fathers. Needless to say, separation from their own children was the heaviest cross for the women to bear for the rest of their lives, since in some cases they were never again to see their offspring.

The Decembrist revolt taught Nicholas I a lesson he was not to forget throughout his lifetime: never again must he experience another confrontation with rebels, particularly if their leaders were of such social prominence as Trubetskoy. He could not forget or forgive a man like Trubetskoy. whose proud name dated back several centuries, for getting mixed up with the rebels. "What was in your head when you associated yourself with that scum?" Nicholas indignantly asked Trubetskoy during the first interrogation. He predicted that a terrible fate lay ahead of Trubetskoy.

When Mme Trubetskaya expressed her desire to join her husband wherever he might be or whatever fate might befall him, both Nicholas I and the Empress tried at first to dissuade her from doing so. After they realized that it was all totally futile and that nothing would sway her determination, Nicholas I said: "Very well! Go ahead! I will remember you!" And the Empress too admired Trubetskaya's will; she declared that she would do all in her power to alleviate her burden in the future.

The harsh and inflexible application of justice in the case of the Decembrists, five of whom were executed and the rest sent into exile and hard labor, testified to the character of the sovereign. Still on rare occasions, Nicholas would display a touch of compassion, demonstrate that his heart was in the right place. Thus, when Pauline Geueble insisted that she wished to go to Siberia to marry the man she loved, the Emperor was deeply touched. He granted her daughter born out of wedlock the right to bear the proud name of her father, Annenkov, and permitted Pauline to deposit in her name at the Moscow bank the money she received from the sale of one of the estates willed to her.[10]

None of the women who volunteered to go into exile with their husbands or beloved had ever demonstrated any political proclivities, entertained any anti-monarchical ideas, or dreamed of even mild reforms. On rare occasions Volkonskaya referred to her husband's past "errors," but that was when she pleaded for some imperial favor. From all the available evidence, it can be safely assumed that none of the women were interested in or even aware of the clandestine societies. What inspired them was marital loyalty, as in the case of Princess Trubetskaya, or their love, as in the case of Princess Marie Volkonskaya, or high moral obligation, as in the case of Pauline Geueble, stimulated no doubt by the presence of an illegitimate child whose father was in Siberian exile.

Governor General A. S. Lavinsky was right in assuming

---

[10] Annenkova, *Zapiski zheny dekabrista*, 135, 136.

in his instructions, issued to Governor I. B. Zeidler, that the women were ignorant of Siberian conditions. They were probably equally unaware of the nature of the political offenses of which their men were accused. Their traditional upbringing and social status precluded involvement in public affairs. To these women the state provided a firm footing, while their religious upbringing gave them an umbrella under which they could find spiritual and moral solace.

As noted, the sacrifice of the women who cast aside all luxury to follow their men into exile touched the heart of poets. The above-mentioned poem by N. A. Nekrasov, "Russian Women," reflected also the prevailing social climate, for it was written in 1871-72, during the period of reforms that followed the Emancipation Proclamation of 1861. It was an era of high hopes and noble expectations, with rising demands for equal rights, an end to sex discrimination, and the granting of equal opportunities for women and men in the field of higher education.[11]

---

[11] Cf. Prince D. S. Mirsky, *A History of Russian Literature. From the Earliest Times to the Death of Dostoyevsky (1881)* (New York: Knopf, 1927), 295-302; V. Pokrovsky, *Zheny dekabristov* (Moscow, 1906), 2-3.

2

Trubetskaya

The Princess Yekaterina (Katasha) Ivanovna Trubetskaya was the first woman to accept the challenge and
follow her husband "to the end of the world if need be."
Katasha, as she was popularly known, was the daughter
of a French emigré, Jean Charles François de Laval de
la Loubrerie, who left France in 1791. He joined the
Russian army and later the Russian foreign service.

In St. Petersburg Laval met Alexandra G. Kozitskaya,
one of the most wealthy women in Russia. When the
couple began to contemplate marriage, the Kozitsky family
showed alarm at the "foreign intrusion." Without telling
her parents, Alexandra appealed directly to Emperor Paul
I for permission to marry. The whimsical Tsar, with characteristic brevity, noted that, as far as he knew Laval was
a Christian and of sufficient rank to marry into the Kozitsky
family. His resolution was simple and brisk: "Marry the
man." And since it was shortly before Lent, he added,
she ought to marry Laval "at once!"[1]

[1] A. Yatsevich. *Pushkinsky Peterburg* (Leningrad, 1935), 150-154.

Sergei Trubetskoy

Yekaterina (Katasha) Trubetskaya

Despite the opposition of the Kozitsky family to having an apostate (*busurman*) as a son-in-law, the imperial decision had to be accepted. In this manner Captain Laval entered the Kozitsky household. He received not only a handsome dowry, but became heir to a good portion of the enormous Kozitsky estate, which included numerous industrial plants in the Ural region as well as real estate elsewhere in Russia. Almost overnight the little known French emigré became heir to fabulous wealth. He established his permanent residence in St. Petersburg and in February 1800 he was named chamberlain at the Court of the Grand Duchess Elena Pavlovna.

The family palace which Laval erected in the most prominent location of the capital, today houses the headquarters of the Central Archives of the U.S.S.R. (*Tsentrarkhiv*). During the early part of the nineteenth century it served as a nucleus of cultural activities in St. Petersburg. It housed outstanding art collections and was a center of social entertainment, with royalty frequently attending the balls. Numerous prominent literary figures frequented the Laval palace.[2] Such was the home that Princess Trubetskaya was forced to abandon in order to spend the rest of her life in exile with her family in distant parts of Eastern Siberia.

Mme Trubetskaya, or Katasha, was a down-to-earth, firm, determined woman with all the qualities and characteristics of her dual ancestry—the dogmatism of the Volga Old Believers on her mother's side, and the rationality of a French winegrower on her father's side. Father Kologrivov admirably and fondly describes her as a "solid, simple and robust" woman, buxom, with a face slightly

---

[2]An up-to-date biographic sketch of Princess Trubetskaya, based on rare documentary evidence, was accomplished by Father Ivan N. Kologrivov. See "Yekaterina Ivanovna Trubetskaya," *Sovremennye zapiski* (Paris), LX, 1936, 206-212.

mutilated by smallpox and a pug nose which, as he put it, was bound eventually to assume the shape of a potato. In appearance as well as manner Katasha carried every sign of that earthy stock passed on by her mother. Moody by nature, yet able to cope with mountainous problems with remarkable sobriety and cool rationalization, she was capable to enjoy life fully, though at times hindered by a touch of melancholia. Outwardly self-centered, she was basically a kind person who often demonstrated an astute response to human suffering. She was unbelievably loyal, highly moral, pious in a genuine sense, and, according to Baron A. Rosen, possessed numerous winning qualities. In later years she became somewhat lumpish in body, though never in mind. Always humane, wise, and sociable, she never allowed a gathering to become leaden. It was not her pock-marked face, but her enchanting voice and level-headed utterances that commanded respect and admiration in the colony of Siberian exiles. Never vindictive or envious and nobly modest, she was admired and respected by all the people who were fortunate to know her.

Katasha met Sergei P. Trubetskoy in Paris. Tall, tan, with curly hair, Trubetskoy spent most of his time abroad, since his father served as Russian minister in Turin. The Investigation Committee later described him as arrogant, vain and faint-hearted, but we may regard the opinion as prejudiced. The career of Trubetskoy seems to contradict such a view. Throughout his lifetime Trubetskoy demonstrated kindness, modesty, and idealism, even though on the fatal day of December 14/26, 1825, his conduct was inexplicably cowardly.

After a short period of courtship Trubetskoy revealed to Katasha that he loved her and proposed marriage. Acceptance of such an offer without parental consent was, of course, out of the question. Early in May the couple, while in Paris, received the eagerly awaited message that the Laval family was happy to accept the offer. Trubetskoy then wrote for confirmation of his engagement to Prince Peter M. Volkonsky, who at that time was accompanying Alexander I to his diplomatic meeting at Laibach. Sergei and Katasha were married in the Russian church in Paris.

Upon their return to St. Petersburg, the young couple resided for a while with the Laval family. Their happiness was mainly derived from the charming atmosphere of their residence, from the generous dowry the family had bestowed on them, and undoubtedly, to no small degree, from the youthful love with which they were both filled. But Katasha had also learned to take in life the bitter with the sweet. Many years later she wrote: "If I have suffered much, if my soul retains bitter regrets, the traces of which will never be ironed out, these were also necessary, for when the Lord sends us sufferings, He does that always for our own good, so that He brings us nearer to Him . . . ."

It was abundantly clear that the marriage of Katasha marked a new phase in her life. Her entire existence came to revolve around her husband; her sole attention focused on a single quest, how to make her marriage meaningful and happy. She began to show less interest in "society," minimized her worries about her appearance, and put less stress on intellectual pursuits than many women of her generation. No thought had entered her mind at this time of the catastrophe that was soon to descend upon them.

The first stunning blow came on the day after the revolt, on December 15/27, when Trubetskoy, who had been arrested, passed a note to Katasha which read: "Do not be angry with me, Katya, I ruined you and myself, without evil intention. The Emperor requests to tell you that I will be alive and in good health." Katasha instantly started to look for permission to have a personal talk with her husband. She was informed that she might send whatever her husband needed; she might also write to him, provided such messages were not sealed and were open for inspection; but she could not see him for the time being.

From this moment on Katasha became almost possessed with the determination to stand by her husband on all occasions and at all cost. What this woman must have gone through during the coming months, while the investigation and trial were in process and Trubetskoy was held incommunicado, can only be imagined. Her only consoling partner was her sister, Zinaida, who was married to Count Gustav Lebzeltern, the Austrian minister to St. Petersburg, and with whom Katasha lived during these crucial months even though it placed the Austrian minister in a particularly awkward position. Picture a representative of the Metternich government harboring under his roof the wife of a leading rebel under arrest and investigation!

The first meeting between Trubetskoy and his wife was granted Easter Monday. It was a moving rendezvous which proved one thing—come what may, no force would be able to keep them apart. While five of the Decembrists were hanged, Trubetskoy was spared despite the fact that some military men had recommended that he and Volkonsky be included among those sentenced to death.

On July 16, three days after the execution of the five Decembrist leaders, Katasha wrote to her husband in prison that she was firmly determined to go with him wherever he might be sent. Opposition to her decision on the part of her parents was expected, not as forceful as in the case of some other families. The Lavals were bitter that Trubetskoy should have brought upon their daughter such a calamity. For the rest of his days Count

Laval deeply resented the unexpected tragedy that had suddenly befallen his family, though he nurtured his feelings in bitter silence. In all the future correspondence with Katasha, Laval significantly ignored Trubetskoy.

3

Departure Eastward

To decide never under any circumstances to be separated was far simpler than to carry out the bold resolution. At first it became necessary to obtain permission from the Emperor, an almost insurmountable task in itself. Yet when Katasha saw her husband on July 16, she assured him that they would be in Siberia together.

A week later Trubetskoy departed for Siberia, placed in iron chains and accompanied by gendarmes, in the first group of state criminals sent into exile. Next day Katasha left her palatial home in St. Petersburg and headed in the same direction, having obtained permission to follow Sergei. She was accompanied by her mother as far as Moscow, while the faithful Swiss secretary of Count Laval, Charles Vaucher, readily consented to remain with Katasha until she joined her husband. Count Laval himself sulkily remained in St. Petersburg, and Katasha was never to see her father again.

Katasha left her home with mixed feelings of despondency and momentary flares of exaltation. She experienced a gnawing feeling at the thought of leaving behind her

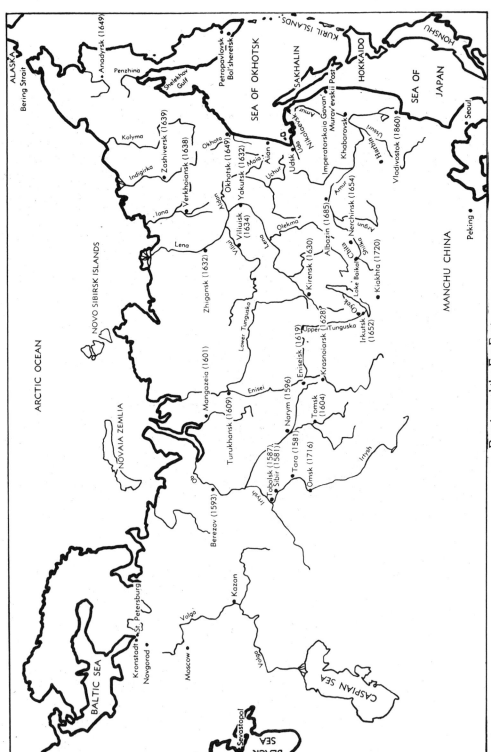

Russia and the Far East

countless memories of childhood, of a happy youth, of domestic comfort, of kind parents and genuine friends. But there was also the inspiring anticipation to be with her husband who needed her more than ever during these sorrowful days, who was impatiently waiting for her arrival, despite his sense of guilt that no one but himself had brought her to this turn of events. At times she felt a bit confused, torn between regrets of what she had to leave behind and exultation that her heroic decision was preordained in order to test her faith, by overcoming whatever her husband had to go through. It was a test of her moral stamina, of her ability to honor the pledge that she had made, to stand together "till death do us part."

Nicholas I was skeptical from the start about the wisdom of permitting women to follow their exiled husbands. There was creeping suspicion that this generosity might be misinterpreted; that it would allow the criminals the comfort of sociability and the convenience of family ties. He feared that the wives might become instrumental in establishing communication links between the exiles and as yet undiscovered seditious elements left behind. The women might also contribute to the legend of martyrdom of the rebels. Nicholas I did not want this to happen; he feared martyrs. He was determined to uproot Decembrism with all the might of his divinely ordained power. Yet he was too God-fearing to render asunder the family, an institution sanctified by the Church and to inflict injustice upon heroic women who chose to honor their marriage vows.

Katasha proceeded to Irkutsk, a distance of some 4,000 miles, by horse-drawn coach, travelling day and night, in spite of cold, fever, and the danger of highway robbery. Speed was of the essence because the fall season arrived early in Siberia, and rains, floods, and impassable roads could soon block her way. When her coach broke down, Katasha continued her journey in a four-wheel peasant cart without springs. Katasha reached Irkutsk by the end of September. The first phase of her ordeal seemed at an end. As she approached the city, Katasha kept crossing herself, thanking her guardian angels for a safe journey, grateful to divine power for reaching the location where she expected at last to see her husband again. A new chapter was about to open in her life.

Trubetskoy had arrived in Irkutsk at the end of August and had been assigned to the nearby salt mines. He expected the arrival of Katasha and counted the hours when he could catch at least a glimpse of her. Theirs was a most tender reunion, accompanied by embraces, reminiscences, and tacit or whispered utterances. One thing was clearly understood: the past was far removed, faded into an indistinguishable gray mist of bygone years. The present was grim, the future uncertain. Yet so long as they could face it together, hope kindled the hearts of both.

At Irkutsk administrative difficulties began anew for Katasha as for the other women who were soon to follow. To have a better understanding of the nature of the recurrent conflict, it is necessary to digress briefly to explain the origin of the perplexing administrative problems the local governor had to face.

When in July 1826 the government sent the convicted Decembrists east, it was unable to issue any specific directions or to give even general indications where the exiles were to be kept. The governor of Irkutsk was compelled to distribute the prisoners on his authority. Some of them he placed at the salt mines of Usolsk. Trubetskoy and Volkonsky were assigned to the Nikolayevsky salt mines. Others were sent to the Alexandrovsk distillery. For this the governor got into serious trouble, because Nicholas I believed that the Decembrists must not be scattered, but kept together at a place like Nerchinsk. However, Nerchinsk did not have adequate accommodations for such a large group, and the governor was not sure how the problem should be solved.

To correct the governor's error in breaking up the group, the government in St. Petersburg contemplated moving the Decembrists beyond Lake Baikal to such a place as the Blagodatsk mines and to keep them under the most stringent rules, removed from the public eye. But Blagodatsk, like Nerchinsk, lacked quarters for such a large group. It was decided, therefore, to locate the convicts temporarily in the old prison near the town of Chita, while hastily constructing special quarters for them near Nerchinsk. Thus in the fall of 1827 the Decembrists were gathered from all the mines and other assigned places and removed to Chita.

When Katasha learned about this decision, she immediately sent a plea to governor I. B. Zeidler, asking him to issue permission for her to follow her husband to the new location. Baffled already by numerous uncertainties and official displeasures in consequence of his former decisions, the governor was completely at a loss what to do with the annoying request. He resorted, therefore, to dilatory tactics. He dwelled at length on the great dangers that such a trip would entail. When Katasha was not intimidated thereby, Zeidler explained in a semi-parental, semi-official manner that life for a respectable woman in that part of the world was most hazardous, particularly in the presence of so many wandering desperadoes and former convicts. He pointed out that she would not be able to secure the necessary protection, or to enjoy the privileges and comforts granted to her in Irkutsk. Nor would she be able to employ servants or to find suitable living quarters. As Nekrasov summed up the governor's warnings in his poem:

> I would have you know, Princess,
> What fate awaits you there.
> The lands down here poor harvest bring.
> But there—no life is seen,
> A shorter spell than our their spring,
> Their winters thrice as keen.
> Eight months of arctic cold they stand,
> What will that mean for you?[1]

When Katasha brushed aside the governor's arguments with the declaration that nothing could be as grim as life without her husband, Zeidler informed her in a more somber tone that in such a case she would have to sign a paper in which she would voluntarily abandon all privileges to which she had formerly been entitled by virtue of her noble rank. Furthermore, she would have to give up all claims to property rights, whether presently owned or claimed by inheritance. Katasha immediately accepted these conditions and signed the required papers.

The document read in part:

> A wife who follows her husband into exile and con-tinues conjugal relations, becomes, naturally, implicated in the fate of her husband. She thereby loses her former status, that is, henceforth she is to be known only as the wife of an exiled prisoner and accepts the bearing of responsibilities imposed upon her husband. Not even authorized persons would be able to render her pro-tection against offenders or prisoners, that dissolute and miserable lot that regards the wife of a state crim-inal as their equal. Offenses may even assume the nature of physical attacks. Punishment does not intimi-date these inveterate criminals.[2]

[1] N. Nekrasov, *Russian Women,* tr. by Juliet M. Soskice, Oxford University Press, 1929.

[2] Cited by Ivan Kologrivov, "Knyaginya Yekaterina Ivanovna Trubetskaya," *Souremennye zapiski* (Paris), LXI, 1936, 234.

The signing of the document by Katasha was no guarantee of her immediate departure. The approaching winter forced her to wait until Lake Baikal was sufficiently frozen to permit safe crossing. But by the middle of September, 1827, the Decembrists and shortly afterwards their wives were on the road to Chita.

In November Katasha's "guardian angel" Sergei wrote to her that she should not expect any comforts at the new location: the hut in which they had lived at the previous location seemed like a palace compared with the "crowded, low, poor shacks" at Chita. He warned Katasha of a total absence of simple accommodations at the new location. It was a far cry from the Laval palace in St. Petersburg!

The distance between Irkutsk and Chita was approximately 400 miles. Road conditions were primitive and hazardous. What little food could be found was unappetizing, unsavory, and unsanitary; it made Katasha ill. But dreariness and exhaustion were almost forgotten when Katasha, upon arrival, found Alexandra G. Muravieva waiting.

Muravieva conveyed to Katasha greetings from many friends, among them the salutations of the poet Pushkin, who sent to the prisoners his famous poem "The Message," which read in part:

> Deep in the Siberian mines,
> Keep your patience proud;
> The bitter toil shall not be lost.
> The rebel thought unbowed.
> . . . .
> The heavy-hanging chains will fall,
> The walls will crumble at a word;
> And Freedom greet you in the light,
> And brother gives you back the sword.[3]

---

[3]Quoted by permission of the translator, Max Eastman.

The Laval Residence in St. Petersburg

Home of Katasha and Marie in Chita

The Decembrist community began to form in earnest with the arrival of other members, followed soon by their wives. Within a short period of time there came to live not far from each other such distinguished members as Trubetskoy, Volkonsky, Obolensky, Yakushkin, Davydov, Artamon Muraviev, and the Borisov brothers. The hardships and adversities were slowly forced into the background, as the new way of life gradually imposed new priorities. In the immortal words of Tibullus, "Hope tells us tomorrow will be better."

Upon the arrival, Katasha immediately requested a rendezvous with her husband. She was allowed to see him the following day for one hour. The next problem was a place to live. Katasha managed to settle in a small and barely furnished hut. Volkonskaya, who arrived a few days later, accepted residence with Katasha. They slept on a hastily made mattress stretched on the floor. The heating was primitive, and the hut was usually smoky. In this household the women managed to concoct various meals to take to their husbands and occasionally to other prisoners, barely subsisting themselves. They shared happy moments while visiting the prisoners, proudly offering their culinary accomplishments or sharing the modest gifts they received from home occasionally.

With the arrival of other wives, the women formed a circle of friends that shared a common devotion. Their dedication touched even the heart of Nicholas I, when he learned about the lives of these noble women. *"C'était un trait de dévouement digne de respect,"* he remarked on one occasion.

The moral support that the presence of the women rendered to the prisoners can hardly be estimated. The labor in the mines and the strenuous working conditions made life more difficult by the presence of all sorts of insects which not even a burning body-rub of turpentine could repell for long, not to mention the heartless attitude of the head of the mines, S. Burnashev. To witness the men going through all this made the wives truly "women of compassion."[4] Burnashev may be judged by one of his casual observations—his regret that administrative regulations compelled him to guard the health of the prisoners, for otherwise he would have "gotten rid of them within a couple of months."

The actual labor demanded of the men at the Chita prison was not excessive, but the physical conditions of men like Trubetskoy or Volkonsky, who showed symptoms of tuberculosis, caused considerable concern. Some men were required to do road work, others labored at the local flour mill; some tended the prison gardens or repaired flood damaged areas.

At the same time, the Decembrists sought to raise the cultural level of the local population in this distant, little Siberian community. They felt that it was their duty to aid the elimination of illiteracy, introduce books, cultivate reading habits, and set up a semblance at least of schools. In the words of M. S. Lunin, one of the most militant Decembrists. "Here, called by fate, the men could by thought and deed contribute to the cause to which they had dedicated themselves originally."

In the drab Siberian life, constantly in the shadow of the prison wall, the single ray that illuminated the life path of Katasha was her ability to see her husband, be it in the prison yard or during the assigned rendezvous. As she wrote to her sister Zinaida in 1829: "You cannot imagine, but since the time I am able to see Sergei, I am calm and contented. I am no more in need of commisera-

[4] *Russkaya starina*, II, 1870, 239. See also M. M. Khin, "Zheny dekabristov," *Istoricheskey vestnik*, XII, 1884, 668-669; *Istoriya Sibiri* (Leningrad, 1968), II, 486; Yakushkin, *Zapiski, stati, pis'ma*, 102-103.

tion; I do not think of the past nor of the present."[5] She wrote these lines when the long awaited event had finally occurred, when, as she put it, "the smile in exile" had visited her. In February 1830, she gave birth to a "state peasant" girl, as the law defined the status of a child born in exile.

In July 1830 Katasha wrote her sister how happy she was to be the mother of an adorable baby girl. As she held the baby in her arms, she wrote, she was distressed by one thought, the inability to feed that tiny creature herself. She expressed the hope that her good intentions might repay for her incapacity to feed the baby and that when Sashenka grew up, she would not regret that she was Siberian born, with all the legal disabilities that this entailed. As to other problems, Katasha added, she relied upon divine justice. Yet a gnawing maternal worry shone through her remark: "But who can foretell what the future of a baby born in more favorable circumstances might be? My faith remains in divine mercy."

Explaining that she had come to Siberia for only one reason—for the sake of Sergei—she wrote that if through divine kindness she had become a mother, it was undoubtedly because divine wisdom desired to render solace to Sergei. It was for the same reason that she would not leave the prison as long as Sergei was there. Katasha insisted that she sought no earthly happiness; through faith she was happy to accept whatever His will might be.

In subsequent letters that same summer Katasha informed her sister of her baby; how much she had grown, how she was able to recognize her mother, and other details of maternal and conjugal bliss.[6]

[5] Ivan, Kologrivov, "Knyaginya E. I. Trubetskaya," *Sovremennye zapiski*, LXI, 1936, 258.

[6] *Ibid.*, 260.

Time relentlessly moved on. Little Sashenka was growing and even learning how to read. One winter day Katasha complained in a letter to Zinaida that the climate
was positively brutal, and she shamefully admitted that if
there was anything in the world that she might envy, it
would be people who live in moderate climates. She confessed further that formerly she used to dream of living
in the Crimea where her children might be able to swim
in the sea. Now she had no such hope whatever. Still,
she added with a touch of characteristic fatalism, "the
future was entirely in the hands of the Creator."

At this point she paused for a moment, reread her
sister's letter in which Zinaida described how she was
preparing for the sacrament in the Greek Orthodox
Church while in Naples. This immediately awakened
memories of Italy, of Rome, and other distant places and
experiences. Katasha frankly admitted a few yearning
moments, but quickly recovered and added that she
cherished one consoling thought: the offspring the Lord
had given her was a truly undeserved bounty and supreme
fortune. Again she paused, then added significantly that
the only thing she hoped for was that her children would
never resent the effects of the years in Siberia.

Outwardly there was little change expected in prison
conditions or regulations. Rendezvous were to be continued as before, twice a week. Occasionally the visiting
hours were stretched by the guard who, mellowed by a
few coins, would render a more liberal interpretation of
prison regulations. Short as the visiting hours were or
seemed, they broke the monotony of the days for the
women and the men and sustained them both.

Occasionally the bliss of motherhood complicated
matters. No child was allowed within the walls of the
prison, and someone else had to take care of the child

during the visiting hours. The father could not see his own child during Katasha's visits.

The environmental drabness, the brutal climatic conditions, the dull days all year around were bound to depress the prisoners and their wives. "I seem to feel like an old woman of sixty rather than of forty," Katasha wrote to Zinaida on one occasion. Despite the valorous spirit, the environment sooner or later enervated most of the dwellers in the area. The frequent colds contracted during the fall and winter seasons, the lack of proper heating and clothes, the totally inadequate medical care as evidenced by the extraordinarily high rate of infant mortality, all combined to leave serious physical and mental imprints upon many of this highly cultured group transplanted into an alien surrounding.

As noted above, the government had begun the construction of a permanent prison at Petrovsky zavod or Petrovsk Works, near the city of Nerchinsk, sometimes referred to as Petrovsky ostrog or Petrovsk Prison.[7] High officials anticipated that the more up-to-date penal institution would allow it to make use of the men sentenced to penal servitude in the local mines. By 1830 the Decembrists and their wives began to contemplate their third trek east within less than four years.

[7] The Petrovsk Works or Prison was located near Nerchinsk, in the neighborhood of the iron and silver mines where prisoners sentenced to penal servitude were sent. By the end of the 1820's a newly constructed prison was erected to house the Decembrists. Surrounded by high fences, the prison consisted of sixty-four solitary cells in twelve buildings, separated to prevent the forming of close associations among the prisoners. The cells were dark since through neglect originally no windows had been installed. Only after numerous pleas and administrative pressure did Nicholas I agree to permit installation of small windows in each cell. By 1835 most of the prisoners, having served out their penal servitude, were transferred into a new category of exiles (*ssyl'nye poselentsy*) instead of "hard labor prisoners" (*katorzhniki*). Later many Poles were sent here, after the unsuccessful insurrection of 1863. See George Kennan, *Siberia and the Exile System* (London, 1891), IX, 278-318.

4

On to Nerchinsk

The Decembrists had spent nearly three years in the old Chita prison. The news that they would soon be moved to Nerchinsk raised hopes that their conditions might be improved. The newly constructed prison at Petrovsk, it was believed, would alleviate the most glaring shortcomings of the old structure.

The departure from Chita for Petrovsky zavod, a suburb of Nerchinsk, was scheduled for August 1830. Once again, the women had to appeal for permission to follow their men to the new location. The first woman to start the journey was, as usual, Katasha, accompanied by her baby, followed soon by two others, Muravieva and Davydova. The journey was expected to take approximately a month.

This time the women, one by one, went ahead of the men, on wagons and squeaky peasant carts, loaded with all kinds of recently acquired necessities, kitchen utensils and provisions. After days of merciless jolting, inadequate nourishment, and lack of sleep, the travellers reached their destination. Many of the local inhabitants, mostly former prisoners, gathered to see the "aristocrats" who had come to join the community. The commandant of

35

the prison who met them gave them their mail which had recently arrived for them.

From the letters and newspaper clippings which they received, the Decembrists and their wives learned for the first time of events that had taken place in western Europe—of the revolution in Paris and of the overthrow of Charles I, and other political developments in current history. When they broke out in song to commemorate the fall of the Bastille, the guards were completely baffled, unable to comprehend the reason for the festive mood amidst the grim surrounding.

The commandant of the new prison, General Stanislav Romanovich Leparsky, deserves brief comment. The women of Nerchinsk considered themselves fortunate that during their most trying years they had to deal with a man like Leparsky. On the surface a strict bureaucrat and at times devoid of any humor (See Appendix), he had beneath the cold uniform and icy looks a warm heart.

Leparsky was of Polish origin and Ukrainian birth. A well educated man who spoke French and German fluently, and by virtue of his Jesuit training, knew Latin thoroughly, Leparsky commanded respect among all the Decembrists. By nature a modest man, even kind and sympathetic with the political prisoners, Leparsky distinguished himself for successfully dealing with the Polish revolutionaries in exile in Siberia. A lifelong bachelor, he did all he could to ease the life of the exiles and their wives, whom the authorities had entrusted to him. It was probably thanks to Leparsky that the Decembrists were unfettered even before their arrival at Nerchinsk, or, as someone remarked dourly, stripped of their "iron music."[1]

[1] On Leparsky see: M. N. Kuchayev in *Russkaya starina*, VIII, 1880, 709-724; S. Maksimov, *Katorga i ssylka*, Part III, Chpt. 2; *Russky arkhiv*, VIII-IX, 1870, 1566-63; X, 1870, pp. 1927-1936; Yakushkin, *Zapiski, stati, pis'ma*, 104-06; 118-119; 126-127; 135-136 & passim; N. V. Basargin, *Zapiski* (Moscow, 1872); *Russkaya starina*, XXXII, 1888, 399-400.

Leparsky's reports to St. Petersburg indicate that he made every effort to present things in such a light as to ease the rules and to regulate the daily life of the prisoners in a more liberal way, not an easy undertaking. It was at his initiative that the women were given permission to construct their own homes. This helped to raise their morale, aside from the fact that it granted them a greater degree of comfort and an air of relaxation amidst an alien, if not hostile, prison environment. The first one to take advantage of this privilege was Alexandra Muravieva, who had managed somehow to stash away enough money. The other women followed suit. They labelled the string of huts they erected "Ladies Street" (Damskaya ulitsa), a name by which the street is known to this day.

The new prison did not offer the hoped for improvements. Katasha feared that the inadequate conditions of the new building might prove fatal to the weak health of her husband. Writing on October 5, 1830, that Sergei had entered the "horrible prison" as a sick man, she expressed concern that "dampness, chill and lack of fresh air in the prison in which he is placed, might affect his health further."[2]

No prison is a cheering sight, least of all a nineteenth century Siberian prison. But the preceding expectations led to particular disappointment. The dismal prison consisted of eight separate yards, invisible from the outside, concealed and divided by high picket fences. Most depressing was the totally dark cells which had no windows whatsoever. It is not clear whether the windows had been left out by mistake or by callous planning.[3]

When the women learned of the situation, they at once started to bombard the authorities with pleas and

[2] *Russkaya starina*, III, 1896, 610.
[3] The prison at Petrovsk stood until 1866, when it burned to the ground. See *Istoriya Sibiri* (Leningrad, 1968), II, 467-468.

Ladies' Street, Petrovskii Zavod

appeals to do something about providing light for the prisoners.[4] In the spring of 1831 an order was finally wrenched from the authorities for the installation of windows. But the windows that were built at the very ceiling of each cell were narrow and admitted only a dim ray of light. To look outside the prisoner had to climb on a chair or table. Yet this was far better than no windows at all and the women justly took pride in their accomplishment.

The Decembrist wives formed a colony that served as a vital factor in prison life, as a source of strength, derived from the indispensable companionship they rendered. Aristocrats mingled with persons of humble background without a trace of snobbery or condescension. The Decembrist Vasilii L. Davydov, who was a veteran of the War of 1812, an adjutant of Prince P. I. Bagration, and a member of the Lifeguard, married a girl who had once been a serf of the Potapov family. The women formed a family cemented tightly by common misfortune. Sorrow and happiness were equally shared. The spirit of "togetherness" enabled them to endure all adversities and to survive the trying years of exile.

From time to time the ranks of the exiles were thinned out. The expiration of prison terms and death kept lowering their number. In November 1832, for example, the Decembrist colony mourned the demise of the delightfully dynamic, charming Alexandrina Muravieva.

Alexandrina had left her two sons and a daughter with their grandmother in western Russia in order to join her husband. Among the exiles were also her cousin, A. F. Vadkovsky, and a brother, A. P. Chernyshev. Kind, generous, irresistibly gregarious, high strung, and overactive, she became forever occupied with the care of anyone in distress or need. But the sorrows of life in exile caught up

[4] See appendix, document K.

with her sooner than she had anticipated. First her pre-
maturely-born daughter died, then a long illness befell her
husband to whom she devoted her entire attention. People
began to observe how Alexandrina became more retiring
and occasionally morose. One day, on the way home from
the bedside of her husband, she caught a cold, which soon
led to more serious complications as her resistance was
already gravely undermined. Sensing the approach of
death, Alexandrina one day summoned Katasha to bid
her farewell, kissed her four-year-old daughter, and tried
to console her despairing husband; then she closed her
eyes and within a few moments expired.

Alexandrina was buried in the tiny cemetery adjacent
to the local church. Her grieving husband erected a crypt
and placed an eternal image-lamp on it. When some years
later one of the Decembrists, Pushchin, revisited Petrovsk,
he paid honor to the grave of Alexandrina. He observed
that the lamp was still flickering. It was a guiding star
for travellers nearing Petrovsky zavod, he recorded in his
notes.

Those who completed their imprisonment and hard
labor sentences were assigned to various locations of exile.
In 1833 Naryshkin and his wife moved to Kurgan (Tobolsk
province), taking with them their three-year-old adopted
daughter, Ulyana. A year later the stalwart Fonvizins proceeded first to Yeniseisk, then to Krasnoyarsk.

The departure of the Fonvizins was a hard blow to Katasha, because Mme Fonvizina had bravely stood by her
side throughout these critical years and close friendship
had formed between them. "My heart shrinks as I wait
for next week in view of the departure of the Fonvizins
who are moving to their exile location," Katasha wrote
her sister. "Her departure will be a true misfortune,"
she added.

In 1835 A. I. Odoyevsky was transferred to Ishim (Tobolsk province), leaving his house to one of his close friends, the Decembrist V. I. Steingel. In 1839 A. P. Yushnevsky had left for a locality near Irkutsk. The Trubetskoys thus remained increasingly alone. They became absorbed more and more in their children, ministering their education and seeing to it that they grew up without any "exile effects." As they lavished all their love and tender care upon their offspring, they wondered if their children would forgive them for having brought them into this world in Siberian exile.

Daily life intertwined joyful hours and routine problems. Katasha revealed her truly stoic character, as she showed on many occasions remarkable breadth of compassion, and rarely complained about her health or anything else. She faced adversities with amazing poise and profound faith and came to regard her lot as a preordained test to prove her merits. Her life as well as her correspondence with her sister unfolded a rare humility and inner peace in Katasha. She continued to render moral and material assistance to her husband and on many occasions to others when they called upon her. She silently suffered from many discomforts, particularly from the beastly cold that penetrated the inadequately heated house. Although life seemed more tolerable when the double windows and double floors were finally installed, the cumulative effects of the past had already made deep inroads on her health. She kept aging rapidly.

Throughout the years in Siberia, the prisoners and their women lived by a single hope, that the term of their confinement might be reduced on some special, national occasion. Some even dared to hope that they would live to witness an amnesty proclamation. A few, such as Lunin, dreamed, as Pushkin predicted, that some day

The heavy-hanging chains will fall,
The walls will crumble at a word;
And Freedom will greet you in the light,
And brother will give you back the sword.

It was a lean hope, yet tacitly cherished by many. How else could they have survived the trials of exile? A Manifesto in 1839 actually reduced the sentences slightly, but basically things were unchanged. Trubetskoy could not anticipate complete release, but even exile would be better than hard labor.

A son was born to the Trubetskoys four years before the expected expiration of the hard labor sentence, in December 1835. He was named Nikita. Katasha was ecstatic. The house in which they lived was crowded, but such mundane inconveniences seemed petty. The tiny windows from the hut faced the grim prison walls and the mountain range in the distance. The prison looked like a "muddy hole," and the mountains did not offer any "cheering sight either." Yet the Trubetskoys were together, bound by common hopes.

In one of her letters to Zinaida, Katasha described how the Trubetskoy household spent the days at this stage. They would rise at about seven in the morning, have breakfast at eight, then Sergei would give to Sashenka a lesson in mathematics, reading and writing in Russian. After luncheon, weather permitting, they would go for a walk with the children and visit other children. At four o'clock in the afternoon they would have tea. They would sup at eight, then put the children to bed. After that, Sergei and Katasha would read, talk, and enjoy their privacy. From time to time the wives would get together for an evening, have tea and either read or relax and have a chat.

In 1836 the Laval family met in the old residential palace in St. Petersburg. Zinaida wrote to Katasha, describing the visit and the changes that had taken place since the fateful revolt and Katasha's departure into voluntary exile. Katasha read and reread the letter. As the detailed description vividly brought back memories of St. Petersburg and the sumptuous palace that had been her home, she suddenly burst into tears "like a mad woman." It had never happened before, because she had studiously avoided reminiscing. Now that the memories began crowding in upon her in all the details of the past, she became deeply upset and was unable to control her emotions.

Other events disturbed Katasha emotionally. As more and more Decembrists moved away, the congeniality of the group faded. Among those who left one after another were N. V. Basargin, the Ivashevs, Dr. F. B. Wolfe, P. N. Svistunov, and eventually the Volkonskys, her closest friends. Farewell parties were held each time. There were toasts, followed by tender embraces and tearful memories. Katasha described one such party as "noisy and sad." She concluded her letter characteristically on a note that bordered on the religious mysticism that was beginning to master her entirely. "Up to date," she wrote, "God has never deserted us in most difficult circumstances. Let us hope with all our strength and beseech Him . . . ."

In May 1837 Katasha gave birth to a girl whom she named Zinaida, after her sister. She was becoming increasingly contemplative and became subject to recurrent periods of melancholic depression. Her letters were filled with frequent references to death and to life beyond. As Katasha became pregnant again, she wrote she had serious doubts whether she would be able to survive another delivery. For this reason, she stated, she was doing everything in her power to be prepared to face the Creator and to die without regrets. It was her wish to express all her sentiments while she was still alive, to tell people how dearly she loved them. The forthcoming maternal felicity was accompanied by ever more frequent moments of despair. In September 1838 she gave birth to a boy, christened Vladimir.

The happy occasion was marred by awareness of the effect that age was having upon her. It brought about a change in some of Katasha's views and values. But one sentiment remained unaltered — her all-embracing love of Sergei.

In October 1839 the long awaited hour had arrived — at long last. Trubetskoy had completed his sentence of hard labor and was to be sent elsewhere, to live with his family in exile. The assigned location was a village, called Oyek, some twenty miles from Irkutsk. The Volkonskys and other Decembrists lived about five miles from the village. As Katasha was about to leave, she mailed some sketches of Petrovsk to her sister, remarking in a note that as she looked at these sketches, she thought of the sorrows and the few happy moments that were associated with the locality.

They were leaving after thirteen years, Katasha wrote, with a sense of gratitude for one thing: that no matter where they found themselves, they never lost hope that He would always protect them and grant them peace. She penned these words precisely sixteen years to the day of her departure from St. Petersburg.

Behind the Trubetskoys was the hard-labor prison term, the callous administrative regulations, and the daily restrictions. Ahead of them now was the promise of retreat to some obscure Siberian village and, God willing, a breath of freer air. But the move to Oyek turned out to be disappointing. On their way to the new domicile, their three-year-old Vanya became ill and died in Irkutsk. To Katasha this was not only a source of personal grief, but a sign of further tragedy. She continued the journey with an agonizing sense of loss and with forebodings of new sorrow ahead. As A. F. Vadkovsky wrote after seeing Katasha in Irkutsk: "I found the Princess depressed, but what was far worse was that she was not only depressed, but indifferent."

Amidst the humdrum of settling down at Oyek, Katasha found time to write to her sister abroad. She informed Zinaida that her family was residing temporarily in a peasant hut, where the main problem was lack of space. She wrote that "the children have no room to run around, no place to move, and we all crowd in to such an extent that we are unable to find any serious occupation or undertake any task that requires time."

A more adequate home was meanwhile being planned by Trubetskoy. To be sure, it could not be an imposing structure, only a small place, but it would be conveniently located and Katasha cheerfully anticipated that it might at least be warm. By April, the third house of the Trubetskoy family since the beginning of their exile to Siberia was sufficiently completed to allow them to move in. At the same time, they received the good news that Mme Laval, Katasha's mother, had been granted permission to send them a governess, a certain Mlle Kuz'mina. The lady soon reached Oyek and within a matter of days adjusted herself sufficiently to become a genuine friend and useful aid to the family.

With their settlement at Oyek, the material conditions of the Trubetskoys unexpectedly worsened, due in part to Katasha's excessive generosity. She spent the family allowance without planning.[5] Consequently she was compelled to cancel her subscriptions to books and magazines, a considerable sacrifice on her part considering

[5] See *Russkaya starina*, XXXII, 1888, 399.

the cultural isolation. "I must say," she wrote, "that books of exclusively literary character have ceased to interest me. Mysterious female characters or thirty and forty-year-old women bore me or are distasteful to me. At my age I am attracted to more serious topics. When I come across a religious theme, a good history, or a biography of some saint, it appeals to me and I read it with enthusiasm or find in such books enormous satisfaction."

In Oyek, as in former places, Katasha soon came to personify kindness and generosity. Not only political exiles, but the entire community came to respect and admire the princess for her unselfishness and for the numerous favors she showered upon people. The recollections of various people praised Katasha for her undiminishing interest in human affairs, her Olympian patience, saintly sympathy with human suffering, and her keen intuition that emanated mostly from her profound religiosity and personal suffering. In Katasha's own words: "The Lord came to me unexpectedly first so that I would be able to come to Him . . . . It was only through trials and sorrow that I began to see things clearer. All this and nothing else placed me on the road to salvation and emancipated me from all sorts of obstacles one usually faces in life."

When her sister in one of her letters recalled some episodes from childhood, Katasha wrote back: "My entire youth appeared alive before me. To think of the past always deeply disturbs me. I love reminiscing and always come to the thought that the Lord must have favored me. I am able to do all this and I am thankful to Him for everything I was enabled to do. As to my sons, particularly my dear deceased Nikita, I can only imagine him among the angels praying for all of us."

Nikita had died in Oyek from scarlet fever, as had his little sister, Kitushka—in June 1843. Katasha gave birth

to another boy, whom she named Ivan, after the grandfather. A year later she bore another daughter, Sophia.
Katasha wrote Zinaida that though her health had improved, she was conscious of advanced age and a sense
of rapidly declining strength. She felt like an old woman
and was unable to use her limbs.

Ill health made death seem nearer and often had a
devastating emotional effect upon her. The status of her
children also depressed her. As mentioned already, the
law stripped children of "state criminals" born in Siberia
of former parental ranks and classed them as "state
peasants." It was a distressing thought to Katasha.

In February 1842, on account of the marriage of the
heir apparent, Alexander Nikolayevich, a manifesto "concerning children of state criminals born in Siberia" was
made public. It provided that girls at an established age,
if their parents so desired, could attend government schools
for the nobility *(Institut blagorodnykh devits)*. Male children of mature age could attend military schools. Upon
graduation and evidence of ability and moral superiority
these young men could get back their hereditary rank, but
not their old family names. They would be known only by
their patronymic. Thus, the son of Sergei Volkonsky would
be named Sergeyev. The imperial manifesto, which com-
menced with a magnanimous gesture ended with a pro-
vision from which most of the parents recoiled.

Only one of the Decembrists, V. L. Davydov, who resided in Krasnoyarsk, took advantage of the manifesto.
Pressed by material circumstances, he realized that he
would never have the opportunity to educate his large
family properly. (He had left four children in St. Petersburg
and had fathered five children in Siberia.) For the sake of
their education he agreed to sign away their right to bear
his family name.

All other Decembrists firmly turned down the offer. With dignified restraint Muraviev, Trubetskoy and Volkonsky rejected the scheme. N. M. Muraviev argued that there was a wide gap between the gracious gesture of the heir apparent and the Christian concept of family life. To deprive a daughter of her surname, for instance, would be a perplexing imposition upon an innocent creature and would cast undeserved shadow upon the memory of her mother.[6]

Trubetskoy was indignant and far less tactful. In a letter to Zinaida he angrily stated that "a child taken away from us to be placed in a state institution is dead as far as we are concerned!" And in his reply to Governor Rupert he bluntly stated that he was deeply touched by the attention given by the heir apparent to the children of exiled parents. But, he continued:

> I dare to trust the Emperor, his kindness will not permit to stamp the mother with the undeserved blot and deprive the children of their family or father's name, as if they were illegitimate.
>
> As to my consent to place my children in a state institution, I, in my state, am unable to dare to take upon myself the decision of their fate. However, I am unable to conceal the fact that detachment of the daughters from their mother would serve as a death blow to the latter.[7]

Volkonsky presented the same argument to Governor Rupert and added that a mother's life was so tied to the lives of her children that the very idea of separation was bound to become a source of alarming anxiety. In that case, he added, could there be any thought of winning favors at the expense of additional suffering or of risking

[6] S. G. Volkonsky. *Zapiski* (St. Petersburg, 1902), 485.

[7] S. P. Trubetskoy. *Zapiski* (St. Petersburg, 1907), 119-120.

the very life of the mother? Therefore, he concluded, he had to beg to be excused from entrusting his children to the government. It would constitute, he said, a breach of the sanctity of the institution of marriage.

Governor Rupert's reaction was characteristic. His bureaucratic mind was incapable of comprehending genuine paternal feeling. Reporting back to St. Petersburg regarding the rejection of the "sincere and noble intention of the government," he added that royal kindness and sympathy "did not find a response in the heart of these cold inveterate egotists."[8]

The insensitive comment should not surprise anyone familiar with the governor's character. An able military man, he was extremely limited intellectually. He towed the official line, was amoral in his attitude, lacked any parental feelings or family principles. Small wonder that eventually he became involved in an administrative scandal and was forced to retire.

In 1845 Nicholas I allowed Mme Trubetskoy and her children for reasons of her health to reside in Irkutsk. Trubetskoy, at the same time, was allowed to visit his family from time to time. The permission was won only after long and complicated appeals by Countess Laval, who argued that her daughter was in urgent need of medical care which could only be procured in Irkutsk.

In granting the appeal of Countess Laval, Nicholas also gave permission for Trubetskoy's daughters to attend the Girls' Institute in Irkutsk. This proved to be particularly welcome, because the head of the Institute was no other than the former governess of the Trubetskoy family, Kuz'-mina. The Empress herself had summoned Kuz'mina before her departure for Irkutsk, and had requested her

---

[8]Volkonsky. *Zapiski*, 487. S. Volkonsky, *O Dekabristakh. Po semeynym vospominaniyam* (Paris, n.d.), 89.

to pay particular attention to the Trubetskoy girls. The schooling turned out to be more satisfactory than had been anticipated. Encouraged by the general development, Katasha wrote to her friend: "We moved to the city of Irkutsk and my husband, with the permission of the governor, is able to visit us from time to time. Fortunately, this turns out to be a sheer formality, since in fact he seldom goes back to Oyek, that is all."

By a stroke of fortune the Volkonskys were able to move to Irkutsk and find a house near the Trubetskoys. Their son was allowed to attend the local gymnasium. The Trubetskoys and the Volkonskys renewed their old neighborly friendship and frequently exchanged visits. Their children too became close as they attended school. For a while Katasha was radiant, then fate once more marred her happiness. Her thirteen-month-old Sonya contracted dysentery and after an illness of only three days died. Once more Katasha buried her child, resigned to the consoling thought that "He took the child to Himself."[9]

Efforts of Countess Laval to obtain permission for Katasha to return to St. Petersburg even for a brief period of time to visit her ailing father failed. In the spring of 1846, Count Laval died. The news, though expected, shocked Katasha. She was worn out by the many death tidings and frequent depressions.

Life in Irkutsk was far better than at Petrovsk or Oyek. Yet rules concerning the status of the exiles remained rigid, at times senseless, and were often applied with total disregard to the nature of the violation. Many of the officials were arbitrary, discourteous, offensive, and rude. Thus, when Princess Volkonsky took her daughter to the

[9] Of the twenty-five children born in the Decembrist families in Chita and five in Petrovsk, seven died prematurely. Of the remaining eighteen, four died of various causes ascribed to climatic conditions, inadequate medical care, or general primitive conditions.

theater, she was curtly informed that "wives of state criminals were barred from attending public entertainment
places." The same happened to Trubetskoy, who was told
after a concert that state criminals were proscribed from
attending such events.

Other exiles had similar experiences. Naryshkina, the
wife of one of the Decembrists, wrote that officials were
nagging her about the attendance of public entertainment
places. "There were moments," she wrote, "when I was
unable to accept this as I should have. All this caused me
a lot of irritation and at times even moments of real fury.
To avoid serious consequences I turn to other things. In
the end, thank God, I would calm down and feel only
sadness and humiliation within me, which proves helpful
and serves as a saving grace. We live very much to our-
selves here, see no one, visit the Girls' Institute where
our children are being educated."

With the appointment in 1847 of the former military
governor of the province of Tula, N. N. Muraviev, as
Governor of Eastern Siberia events took a more favorable
turn. Muraviev (1809-1881), later known as Muraviev-
Amursky, was a practical and talented administrator. Aside
from his utilitarian handling of the administrative problems, he initiated a new relationship between officialdom
and the political exiles. Some of the Decembrists Muraviev
knew through relatives, others through friends. He did
not have the authority to restore their civil rights or freedom, but he did everything in his power to improve their
lot and to utilize their intellectual and educational abilities.

Muraviev's arrival on the scene as governor marked a
noticeable change in the dull provincial atmosphere of
Eastern Siberia. Casting aside the stiff formality of former
days, Muraviev began to receive some of the exiles at his
residence. Indeed, the governor and his wife even initiated

unprecedented visits to the homes of some of the Decembrists. Muraviev soon established particularly friendly
relations with the Trubetskoys and the Volkonskys. When
the English traveller Thomas W. Atkinson some years
later visited Irkutsk, he reported:[10]

> At the time of my visit to Irkoutsk there were six of
> the exiles still living in the town, viz., Prince Volkonskoi,
> Prince Trubetskoy, and Colonel Pogge [A. V. Poggio],
> with their families; the others were Mokhanoff [P. A.
> Mukhanov], and two brothers Borisoff [Andrei and
> Piotr Borisov]. These formed the best society in Irkoutsk,
> and some of the most agreeable days which I spent in Si-
> beria was in enjoying the intercourse with them. They are
> now living in comfort, mixing in society, and gathering
> around them all the best that Irkoutsk afforded. The
> Princess Trubetskoi has spent several of her youthful
> years in the kingdom. She was a clever and highly
> educated woman, devoted all energies to the education
> of her three daughters and a young son, and was the
> first lady who followed her husband into Siberia. I
> heard from her own lips an account of her journey
> through those dreary regions, when she was attended
> only by a maid-servant, as well as of her reception and
> treatment when at the mines of Nerchinsk. The Princess
> Volkonskoi was the next to follow; she had a son and
> daughter; the latter was one of the most beautiful girls
> I ever beheld. Both these families possessed every
> thing they could desire, except liberty to return to their
> homes; with the others it was different, and with two
> of them it was indeed a hard struggle for existence.[11]

The death of little Sonya (Sophie) of dysentery, followed soon by the death of her own father had jolted
Katasha badly. A picture she sent to her sister showed
how she had deteriorated physically. Distraught, Zinaida

---

[10] Thomas W. Atkinson. *Travels in the Regions of the Upper and Lower Amoor and
the Russian Acquisitions* (New York, Harper & Bros., 1860), 303.

[11] See appended Biographical Data.

commented: "Aging and gaining so dreadfully! To let yourself down so much!" Katasha herself had to admit that she was growing fat, though not so badly as the picture might suggest (February 1846). "In general," she explained, "I have the appearance and habits of an old woman, and I do feel terribly aged." She added that her husband, Sergei, had been aging rapidly too, and that his hair had turned completely white. Life in exile scarred many, rejuvenated few. The tawdry daily life of imprisonment, of exile, of civil confinement, all combined to leave deep imprints upon every one, men or women.

Katasha's health kept sagging rapidly, though she would rarely speak of it. She was ailing throughout the entire spring and summer of 1854. Though she suffered a great deal, hardly anyone was aware of what she was going through. Even her doctor was not cognizant of the gravity of her illness.

During the night of October 14, Katasha asked for a priest and on the following morning, as she would have said, "joined the angels."

Katasha had died of cancer at the age of fifty-four. She did not live to see the amnesty that Alexander II was to issue two years later.[12] After waiting for such an amnesty for almost three decades, she expired on the threshold of freedom.[13]

The death of Katasha dazed Trubetskoy and left him a broken man. He felt totally forsaken. The children too were stunned and wept quietly during the funeral cere-

[12] See *Polnoye sobranie zakonov,* No. 30883, xv. The amnesty of August 1856 did not restore freedom completely to the Decembrists. They were permitted to return to western Russia under certain restrictive conditions. For instance, they were forbidden to reside either in Moscow or in St. Petersburg; they were also to remain under police surveillance. The Decembrists protested the surveillance most strenuously on various occasions, but without effect. (See *Diela i dni,* I, 1920t 410-413. Also *Sibirskie ogni,* V, 1924, 152-154)

[13] See B. G. Kubalov, "Dekabristy i amnistiya," *Sibirskie ogni,* V, 1924, 143-159.

mony. The burial was simple, as befitted the character of the deceased. The people who had gathered witnessed the drama without so much as a whisper. As one of the participants later observed: "The princess did not need funeral orations or public praise. Her life spoke for itself. The people who attended the burial ceremony and who during her lifetime had benefitted just from knowing her, brought with them simply their love and their tears within their hearts."

Three years later Trubetskoy wrote in a letter that there was no more happiness for him, since the one who had shared his life's moments of joy and days of sorrow was no more at his side.[14]

In the private collection of A. V. Davydov, a descendant of the Decembrist V. L. Davydov, there is a well-preserved portrait of Katasha made during the late period of her life. It shows an affable face in a modest attire, with a common cap as headgear, and with a shawl held by graceful, slightly swollen hands. The serene face radiates a keen mind, while her expressive eyes reveal the gift of intelligent listening and of provocative conversing. Her letters of later years betray a condition of poor health of which she reluctantly wrote to her sister. Only through oblique hints was one able to detect her declining physical state which during the last years began to deteriorate more rapidly. Her limbs, she rarely admitted, refused to serve her as in former years, while during the last few years she was forced to resort to a wheel chair even in the house. Despite her serious condition, there were practically no allusions to be found in her correspondence to her handicaps. Only on rare occasions would she admit of her silent suffering, of her inability to move freely.

[14]I. Kologrivov, "Knyaginya E. I. Trubetskaya," *Sovremennye zapiski* (Paris), LXII, 1936, 279.

It was only after her death that the silent bearing of pain assumed an illuminating feature of her character.

While the old generation was fading from the scene, the younger one, born and raised in Siberia, began to scatter as it reached adulthood and became alienated from or indifferent to the views of its parents. Liza, the charming daughter of the Trubetskoys, married an army officer and moved away. She was soon followed by her sister, Alexandra, who was married and shortly afterwards moved to the Sino-Russian border town of Kyakhta. By the time Zina became engaged, Katasha was no longer among the living.

Among the first to return to western Russia after the proclamation of the amnesty was Volkonsky, soon followed by Trubetskoy. Before his departure Trubetskoy went to the Znamensky monastery where Katasha was buried, to pay his last respects to her. He stood at the grave for a few minutes, nearly fainted, and had to be helped to the waiting cart.[15]

By special permission Trubetskoy looked forward to spending his last years with his daughter in Moscow. Then in June 1860, he learned that his favorite daughter Alexandra had died of tuberculosis, leaving three children. This was a shattering blow to Trubetskoy, and several months later he himself died of apoplexy. Only one daughter of the entire Trubetskoy family lived long enough to witness the revolution. She was Zinaida Sergeyevna, who resided in the city of Oryol, where she died without notice in June 1924.

The last offspring of the Decembrist Trubetskoy family passed away while a new Russia was barely emerging from the revolution and the civil war. The country did not resemble what her father had envisioned in St. Peters-

[15] B. G. Kubalov, "Dekabristy i amnistiya," 154.

burg a century before or through the years in Siberia. It was a totally different dictatorship from the one the Decembrists had romantically visualized when they had groomed Trubetskoy as "dictator"! But, as Karl Marx has observed, though men try to make history, there are always unintended consequences to any action regardless of plans or predictions.

5

Marie Volkonskaya

Princess Marie Volkonskaya was as determined as Katasha Trubetskaya to share her husband's exile, even if it meant going to the end of the world.[1] The parents of Marie were as unhappy as the Lavals with their daughter's decision. Her father, General N. N. Rayevsky, who tacitly disliked Volkonsky, believed that his daughter was under the influence of that "nasty man" who encouraged her to follow him to Siberia by praising her as the heroine of the day, by praising her courage and flattering her ego. The parents of Marie feared that the Volkonskys instilled in Marie the feeling that she was destined to assume the role of martyr. When the Rayevskys finally and dourly consented to let Marie go, her mother gave her only enough money to reach Irkutsk; for the rest of the journey Marie had to pawn her jewelry.[2] Yet General Rayevsky

[1] A touching tribute to Marie Volkonskaya may be found in the memoirs of a descendant of the Volkonsky family, based on family papers. See Sergei Volkonsky, *O Dekabristakh. Po semeinym vospominaniyam* (Paris, n.d.), 72-73.

[2] P. Shchegolev, *Istoriya molodoy Rossii* (Moscow, 1908), 65; Volkonskaya, *Zapiski*. 16, 20.

Sergei Volkonsky

Marie Volkonskaya

continued to adore his daughter, even if he was displeased with her conduct. Shortly before his death in November 1829, as he looked at the portrait of his daughter, he admitted that "There was the most wonderful woman I had ever known!"[3]

Marie Volkonskaya was born into the Rayevsky household in 1808. Her father reflected the era through which he had lived. He was a contemporary of the "merry days of Catherine II," a "free thinker of the times of Voltaire," and a war hero of 1812. Noted for his unimpeachable honesty and his valor in battle, he became a national hero. He had an acerbic mind, touched by eighteenth-century rationalism and by irreverence of the French Revolution. Marie's mother was a descendant of M. V. Lomonosov, the celebrated poet and scientist of eighteenth century Russia.

The Rayevskys represented the beau monde of Russian society. Their salon was the gathering place of most of the country's literary luminaries. Here one could meet such eminent figures as the poets V. A. Zhukovsky and A. S. Pushkin who was friendly with Marie's younger brother, Nikolai. Pushkin dedicated many lines of his poems to Marie.[4] The famous lines in Yevgeny Onyegin to her former lover, "But I am given to another, And true to him I shall remain," proved prophetic and applicable to Marie. Marie's brother was noted for his caustic skepticism and keen mind; her sister was married to General M. F. Orlov of the days of Alexander I, later incriminated in the Decembrist movement.[5] The uncle of Marie, L. V. Davydov, was later one of the exiled Decembrists and a popular literary figure during the early 1820's. Such in

---

[3] Russkaya starina, VI, 1878, 338; Arkhiv Rayevskikh, I, 383, 384.
[4] See "Pushkin v yuzhnoi Rossii," Russky arkhiv, 1866, p. 1115.
[5] Anatole G. Mazour, The First Russian Revolution, 74-75; 81-82 passim.

brief was the environment in which Marie Volkonskaya grew up and spent her youth.

Marie was an impressive-looking lady—tall, charming, and energetic—who walked with special grace. She was known in her days as *"la fille du Gange"* because of her impressive black eyes and curly hair. Pushkin once said that her hair was more lustrous than daylight and darker than night, while Baron Rosen referred to Marie's eyes as "conversing." She was barely eighteen when she married Prince Sergei Volkonsky. No one could have foreseen that this carefree princess would soon play such a heroic part in the life of the young prince, or abandon her palatial residence and follow thousands of miles to the eastern border of the empire to be with her husband, the "state criminal."[6]

Prince Sergei G. Volkonsky was a descendant of an old noble family, originally from the Principality of Chernigov. Volkonsky was arrested two weeks after his son, Nikolenka, was born. After the collapse of the December revolt and the pending trial of the participants, there was little thought of what lay ahead for the defendants or their families. Shortly after the trial, Marie revealed few signs of wishing to join her husband in exile. Her first reaction was one of curiosity. Writing to her sister, she merely queried what kind of life the exiled men would face. In another message soon to follow, Marie asked naively: "Will they be confined? This thought troubles me. Will my poor Sergei have at least a small corner of land where he might cultivate a garden? That is all he needs. What do my dear lady-friends of misfortune do?"

Such was the desultory nature of her early notes. From time to time one detects a despairing cry, a sign of resig-

---

[6] *Russkaya starina*, IV, 1875, 822, 823; *Istorichesky vestnik*, V, 1904, 533-534.

nation when desolation begins to master her mind. More often one comes across matter-of-fact queries, plain idle curiosity. Then, as days passed by, the gravity of the situation sank in. She began to inquire where Sergei might be sent, for how long, and what would be the nature of the forced labor imposed upon him. Certain that their daughter would remain behind to take care of her only child, the Rayevskys were shocked when Marie suddenly revealed to them her determination to follow her husband to Siberia.

Whether solely of her volition or influenced by the action of Katasha, Marie decided to join Sergei wherever he might be sent, regardless of objections by her father. Neither administrative obstacles placed in her way nor other impediments could break her will. She was ready to sign any papers presented to her as long as they promised a reunion with Sergei.

With this purpose in mind Marie went to St. Petersburg to appeal personally to Nicholas I that His Majesty grant her the necessary papers. The imperial reply, dated December 21, 1826, was in the spirit of an avuncular warning: She must realize what was bound to be ahead of her, particularly after her arrival in Irkutsk. The Emperor declared that he would leave it to her discretion whether she should follow her husband or remain at home. But she must be fully aware, he reiterated, what lay ahead of her should she decide to join her husband in Siberia.[7]

Marie was given to understand that should she follow her husband, she would thereby renounce the right to return to western Russia. And she would have to leave behind her one-year old son, Nikolenka, as the children of state criminals could not be taken to Siberia. This must have been a most difficult decision. In every letter Marie

[7] Volkonsky, *Zapiski*, 460.

kept inquiring about Nikolenka's health, growth, or interests. She finally left the little boy with the grandmother. She never again saw him, for Nikolenka died in January, 1828. When people admired her composure, Marie would reply somewhat indifferently, "What is so astonishing about it? Five thousand other women voluntarily do the same thing."[8]

While in St. Petersburg, Marie had one of her last encounters with her father concerning her intention to join Volkonsky in Siberia. Little by little Rayevsky began to yield ground, admitting that Volkonsky had only noble intentions and that as 'the father of Marie's child he deserved more sympathetic understanding. Separation might cause damage to both, to Marie and to the child, he thought. But the heart of the old soldier did not easily melt. In a letter to Marie he remarked that her husband deserved the fate and was guilty before the entire family. "Still, he is your husband," he concluded, "and the father of your child. Because of his complete repentance and his feelings toward you, it compells me to pity him despite my indignation. I forgive him as I wrote to him a few days ago."

The farewell party given in honor of Marie was, according to one guest, a "cheerless affair." In spite of songs, music, and lively conversation, there was an air of depression. Stalwart Marie repeatedly maintained that what she had chosen was simple and unheroic and explained it thus: "My son is fortunate, my husband is unfortunate, hence my place is to be with my husband." Yet the poet D. V. Venevitinov, who knew Marie, detected a different inner drama when he wrote the following lines dedicated to her:

[8] P. Shchegolev, "Podvig russkoy zhenshchiny," *Istorichesky vestnik.* V. 1904. 550: *Arkhiv Rayevskikh*, I, 370.

Her source of tears went dry. Resigned to her fate, she resolved to bear in her heart a lifetime burden of sorrow, and for that reason became more serene. She saw in herself supreme virtue, a guardian angel, a harmonizer between two beings of whom she remained the sole survivor in the world . . . . Henceforth she would live in a world she created for herself . . . . In its inspiration she chose her own fate and fearlessly gazed into the future.[9]

There is conflicting evidence that upon her departure for Siberia Marie had not clearly understood her inability to return west. Such at least was Marie's assertion. This might explain her seemingly heedless conduct during those trying days. Her letter from Nerchinsk casts a fuller light on the matter. In 1827 she wrote: "It seems to me that upon my arrival here I gained more wisdom, particularly since passing Irkutsk, where I learned that I may not be able to return. If this is so, I am very fortunate that I did not understand this before.[10] Now I am able to dedicate myself entirely to my husband with a clear conscience. My heart's single desire is to render my obligations and share my life with Sergei and my son. One must have more will power than I to abandon a husband after observing his condition in which he was cast by his own errors. Now I am able to understand what the Emperor meant when he said 'Think of what is awaiting you beyond Irkutsk.' I thank the Lord a thousand times for not understanding this before, otherwise I would have experienced torments that would have torn my heart apart. Now I stand innocent before my child even if I am not with him. At times I visualize how my parents felt when they learned all about this. Only during such moments do I suffer."[11]

[9] *Russkaya starina*, 1875, 822-827.

[10] *Russkie propilei* (Moscow, 1915), I, 20. This is debatable since Marie was given to understand long before, that once she departed from Irkutsk her return to western Russia would be unlikely.

[11] *Ibid.*

The question of children following the mother to Siberia came up on several occasions. When in 1829 the wife of Yakushkin again appealed to the government to allow her and her two sons permission to join the imprisoned husband and father, the request was turned down. The main reason was that the two boys would not be able to receive a proper education in Siberia. Desperate, Mme Yakushkina in 1832 was willing to go without the two boys and appealed to her husband to send her the necessary papers for the trip to Siberia. On April 3, 1832, Nicholas I wrote: "Turn down the request under some plausible excuse." Thus Mme Yakushkina was prevented from going to live with her husband.

Marie's eastward journey was adventurous. Aside from the discomforts caused by the primitive means of transportation, Marie had to overcome numerous administrative barriers. Like the other wives, she had to sign papers listing the conditions she had to accept before she could depart from Irkutsk. The conditions included the following provisions: Rendezvous with her husband were to be held only by permission, on specified days, and with the approval of the commandant. No money, papers, or writing implements could be passed to the prisoners, nor could letters or notes be accepted from them unless authorized. Volkonskaya's belongings must be recorded in the office of the commandant. No beverages of any kind were allowed within the premises of the prison. All rendezvous with the prisoners must be in the presence of the guard and all conversations carried on in Russian only. Finally, Volkonskaya had to pledge not to absent herself from her domicile without informing the senior officer of her whereabouts.[12]

Before Marie set out for Siberia, Nicholas I personally warned her in the hope of dissuading her from joining

[12] S. Maksimov, *Sibir i katorga,* Part III, 205-206. Cited by M. M. Khin, "Zheny dekabristov," *Istorichesky vestnik,* XII, 1884, 659-660.

her husband. While crossing the Ural mountains and then again upon her arrival in Irkutsk, Governor Zeidler, most likely at the suggestion of Nicholas I, made a last endeavor to convince her that she was bound to meet great risks as she proceeded with her journey; she would be much wiser if she returned home. The Governor also informed her of the rules he had cited to Katasha regarding her own status and that of the children she might have in Siberia; he added about the prohibition against taking along money or valuables.

All these conditions meant little to Marie for, as she wrote to her mother later: "Be certain, dear Maman, that there is no such sacrifice that I would not take in order to win the single consolation left on this earth—to share the fate with my husband. The loss of titles or wealth, for me, of course, is no loss at all.[13] What do I need it all without Sergei? What is life to me if it is afar from him? Only in Siberia is one to learn the appreciation of true values in life."[14]

Marie Volkonskaya reached Irkutsk in January 1827. Here she met Katasha and a lifelong friendship developed between them. From Irkutsk they proceeded together to Chita, where they arrived on February 9, 1827, after covering an immense distance in record time. Marie had been only twenty-one years of age and married to Volkonsky for only about three months, when the tragic events had engulfed her young life.

In Chita, Marie and Katasha rented a peasant hut near the prison. It was unusually cold and the low temperature literally numbed Marie, but she immediately began to make arrangements for a rendezvous with Sergei. Three days later—it seemed like an eternity to her—an official

[13] Concerning property rights and other legal aspects see *Istorichesky obzor deyatel'-nosti komiteta ministrov* (St. Petersburg, 1902), Vol. II, Part 1, pp. 78-79.
[14] *Russkie propilei*, I, 1915, 18, 19.

notice reached her that she must once again sign and officially confirm her acceptance of her status as the wife of a state criminal. Marie had no choice but to sign the obtuse bureaucratic document in order to see her husband. As someone said, "A rendezvous was a smile of prison exile."

The long awaited visit was a jolting experience. Marie was shocked by the congestion and the extraordinarily unsanitary conditions in the prison. One section was occupied by the regular prisoners, officially called "recidivist criminals," while the other section across the hall, was occupied by the "state criminals" or, in the language of the "recidivists," the "aristocrat-prisoners." There was a total of eighty-two prisoners in the building. The inmates were placed in small cells with ceilings so low that the prisoner could not stand up straight. Volkonsky shared a cell with Trubetskoy and Obolensky. For a time the prisoners had to wear leg irons that kept irritating the skin of the wearer and annoyed the cellmates with their eternal clanking. Since there were no mines at Chita, the prisoners were assigned all sorts of public chores. They worked at the local flour mill, cultivated the prison garden, attended to sanitation, repaired the buildings or swept the nearby streets.

On February 12, 1827, Marie wrote to her mother that she had finally managed to see Sergei. She found him thin, sickly looking, and pledged that she would not leave him until he had shown improvement. Marie added: "I will not give my son any reason for regret, for I will not return to him unless it is with a perfectly calm conscience even if I would have to wait all fourteen years [of the prison term] . . . . Yes, dear Maman, the more my husband is unhappy the more he can count on me and my attachment to him. I am not angry with my parents that to date they have failed to understand that my only solace is to share the fate with Sergei. I know it is much more difficult to suffer on account of my child than for oneself, therefore I do not permit myself to complain. On the contrary, I am fortunate that I am able to prove that I can fulfill my obligations."[15]

In a letter to her sister, shortly afterwards, Marie wrote that she regarded herself fortunate and entirely self-possessed, mainly because she lived near her husband. "Contrary to everything," she remarked, "my first obligation presently is to be with him, not only to fortify his spirit and his strength. My main concern is his health."[16]

Three days later, Marie wrote to her mother: "We must trust in God, my dear Maman, be ready to accept obediently the new trials which He may send us to make us worthy in the future of His boundless compassion . . . ." The message was portentous. In January, 1828, Marie was informed that her son, Nikolenka, whom she had left behind, had died. The shock was so great that Marie could not recover from it for many months. A year later, she was still affected. "Every day I sense more the loss of my son," she wrote. "I am unable to tell how I feel when I think of our future. When I die, what will happen to Sergei who has no one in this world that might care about him? Certainly no one could be concerned as much as his son."

The death of Nikolenka had removed the last link between the life Marie had left behind and her life in exile. With a touch of despair she endeavored to explain apologetically that in her state of mind the only way to gain inner peace would be in the presence of her husband. Her father's reply must have hurt her feelings when he wrote that, "Not knowing the location of the prison, nor conditions, I would not permit myself to express my views. You

[15] Ibid., 4-5.
[16] Ibid., 12.

may act at the advice of your own mind and heart, but I will have no part of it."

Marie had barely recovered from the shock of Niko-lenka's death, when her father, General N. N. Rayevsky, passed away in September of the following year. On the very same day she lost the baby girl, Sophie, in childbirth. The jolting events left Marie in a state of acute depression. The warnings she had received of the grim land of exile began to assume the nature of a prophetic vision. At the close of 1829 Marie wrote to her mother: "Here is the New Year. It is sad to meet the New Year without expec-tations. Our fate will not be changed. My simple wish is that I will be able to share the prison cell with Sergei."[17]

Marie and Katasha set up household together. They sent their help back home, doing the cooking and the cleaning themselves. Like others, they corresponded with their families and relatives, and as officially requested, submitted their letters to the proper authorities for man-datory censorship. Little by little they either managed to build their own homes, a semblance of log cabins, or rented huts from local inhabitants. Money for the building of their homes or for similar purposes, was sent to them by members of their families through official channels. As noted above, the women lived at Chita nearly three years, until a new prison was completed.

As Marie looked over the countryside of Chita, she sadly remarked in one her letters: "In the entire surround-ing landscape only one native thing can be detected—the grass on the grave of my child.[18] The trauma of her ex-perience in exile left her with an ambivalent characteristic: a romantic subtlety and a practical toughness. Most of

[17] *Russkaya starina*, VI, 1878, 340.

[18] Sergei Volkonsky. *O dekabristakh. Po semeynym vospominaniyam* (Paris, n.d.), 84.

her letters reveal a clearly flaccid manner of writing as as well as a firmness in decision.

The conditions in which her sick husband was confined offered Marie little solace. The dilapidated structure that served as the prison urgently required capital repairs. But these were being delayed because the prison was soon to be abandoned for the one under construction near Nerchinsk.

In 1830 the prisoners and shortly thereafter their wives undertook the trek to Petrovsky zavod, a distance of about 400 miles. When Marie reached the destination on September 30, 1830, she exclaimed, *"Me voilà enfin dans la terre promise."*[19]

Although the women could write home, their letters were rigidly censored by the commandant and other local officials, then by the civil governor. All letters or packages sent to them from western Russia were likewise censored and their contents scrutinized. "My dear Maman, what courage one needs to live in this country!" Marie wrote to her mother. "It is fortunate that we are forbidden to write to you frankly about it."[20]

As noted, the new prison at Petrovsk had unexpectedly bad accommodations. The cells were totally dark. There was a long corridor, about seven feet in width, along the entire building. The window of the corridor faced onto the outside prison yard. The corridor was divided into several sections by walls across its length. Each section contained the doors of five or six cells, and one door that led to the outside yard. The cells had no windows whatever, only small openings over the doors, with iron bars across the openings. The dim light coming through these

---

[19] The reader is recommended an excellent essay on the life of Marie Volkonskaya by O. Popova, "Istoriya zhizni M. N. Volkonskoy." *Zvenya*, III-IV, 21-128.

[20] *Russkie propilei*, I, 1915, 41.

openings reached the cells only if their doors were open; when the cell doors were shut total darkness prevailed.

Commandant Leparsky allowed the wives to live with their husbands in the cells. Those who were childless took advantage of the permission. It was they who then appealed to Leparsky for the installation of windows and Laparsky, after a lengthy correspondence with the government, provided the sixty-four cells with narrow openings just below the ceiling. Only a misty ray of light shone through, but the wives rejoiced in their victory, officially interpreted as an act of "boundless royal magnanimity."[21]

The local administrators and guard officers did not treat the prisoners and their families with any courtesy. One incident deserves mention, for it could have had tragic repercussion. When Alexandra Muravieva visited her husband in his cell one time, the officer on duty, as was the custom, remained in the cell. Since Alexandra was not feeling too well, she reclined on the cot.

As she conversed with her husband in Russian, she threw in some French phrases from time to time. The officer on duty, who was somewhat intoxicated, stepped up and rudely insisted that they speak Russian only. Alexandra missed the meaning of the remark and asked her husband, *"Qu'est ce qu'il veut, mon ami?"* Not understanding French, the guard assumed that she was making some derogatory remark. He grabbed her arm and shouted: "I demand that you speak Russian!" Frightened, Alexandra began to scream and ran out of the cell with the guard in pursuit. When the other Decembrists heard the commotion, they emerged from their cells and seeing Alexandra chased by the guard, grabbed the man to reason with him.

---

[21] See appendix, Letter of Count Benkendorff to E. A. Shakhovskoi.

The inebriated guard shouted to the soldiers to fix their bayonets and to prepare to meet the rebellion. Luckily a superior officer appeared on the scene and removed the excited guard. The prisoners were ordered back to their cells. When the commandant returned to the prison after a short absence, he apologized to Muravieva for the rudeness of the guard, but warned the prisoners to be more careful in the future. The cool head and lenient nature of Leparsky saved the situation. Had it not been for the commandant, the incident might have had severe consequences.[22]

After the women settled down at Petrovsk, some of them constructed their own little houses and their husbands were allowed to visit them from time to time, accompanied by a guard. This was a special favor and gratefully accepted by those who had children or who were ill. The Volkonskys had two children, a boy Michael, born in 1832, and a daughter Elena, born two years later.

Sergei Volkonsky suffered from acute arthritis, which from time to time kept him bedridden. When his hard labor sentence expired in February 1835, the government consented to let him go to Turinsk for two months to take the cure at the local mineral baths.

In considering where the family was to live in exile, the question of education for the children was a factor. When the government decided to leave the family in Petrovsk for the time being, Marie Volkonskaya protested that the Petrovsk schools were inadequate. She appealed to St. Petersburg that the Volkonskys be permitted to reside in the village of Urik, along the banks of the Angara River. Dr. F. B. Wolfe lived there in exile, and the Volkonskys would be able to obtain the medical aid they needed frequently. Marie's request to live in that region was granted and in March 1837 the Volkonskys moved to Urik.

[22] N. V. Basargin, *Zapiski* (Petrograd, 1917), 113-15.

Urik was a wretched village, whose flatland, dry soil, and sparse vegetation were as unattractive as its severe climate. There was only one merit: aside from Dr. Wolfe, the village harbored J. V. Poggio, the Decembrist, who had acquired a small house in which the Volkonskys stopped upon their arrival.[23] Not far from Poggio lived N. Muraviev, who led a lonely and morose life after the death of his wife in Petrovsk. Poggio had been sent here directly from the Schlusselburg fortress, where he had spent eight years in solitary confinement. Here also at one time had resided M. S. Lunin, before his recent punitive exile, to Akatui.[24] In due course the exiles formed a close circle welded by common misfortune. Only the Decembrist D. I. Zavalishin by his strange and inexplicable conduct alienated many members of the colony.[25]

The Volkonskys were compelled to live modestly in Oyek, because for some unknown reason the monthly allowance that reached them through official channels had been reduced to one fifth of the previous amount. This placed them not only in a difficult material position themselves, but limited their ability to assist other needy members, as they were in the habit of doing. They asked their relatives to send them clothes and provisions rather than money. In 1838 Marie appealed to Governor Rupert to increase the allowance sent to them by their relatives, on the grounds that the cost of education of the children

[23] On Poggio see Franco Venturi, *Il moto decabrista ei i fratelli Poggio* (Milan, G. Einaudi, 1956). See also O. Popova, "Istoriya zhizni M. N. Volkonskoy." *Zvenya*, III-IV, 1934. See particularly pp. 116-128.

[24] A nineteenth-century English traveller wrote: "If there is in Siberia a more lonely a more cheerless, a more God-forsaken place than Karā, it is the snowy, secluded valley of Akatui." See also S. B. Okun', *Dekabrist M. S. Lunin* (Leningrad, 1962), particularly pp. 255 ff.

[25] See *Pamiati dekabristov. Sbornik materialov* (Leningrad, 1926), pp. 124-131; S. Ya. Shtraikh, *Dekabrist I. I. Pushchin* (Moscow, 1926), 215, 224, 284; A. E. Rosen, *Zapiski dekabrista* (St. Petersburg, 1907), 156; *Russkaya starina*, IX, 1903, 706-716; X, 1903, 221-239. Cf. *Byloe*, January 1906, 311-317; *Minuvshie gody*, V-VI, 1908, 523.

as well as the general cost of living in Oyek were unexpectedly high. The request was denied as was a new plea the following year. An appeal by Marie's brother on behalf of the Volkonskys also failed to alter the position of the government.

The hopes for a brighter future proved illusory. Sergei's health continued to deteriorate. In 1840 he was permitted to go once again to Turinsk for treatment, remaining there briefly "under proper surveillance." The task of educating the children rested almost entirely on Marie's shoulders. But though she could teach them French and English, other subjects such as geography, mathematics, and grammar required experienced tutors. Marie hoped to send the children to Irkutsk where they might enter the gymnasium. Entrance examinations were strict and called for adequate preparation, which, in turn, required tutoring that could be obtained only in Irkutsk and was prohibitively expensive for the Volkonskys.

Reference to the government offer to take over the education of the children provided they would give up their paternal name has already been mentioned. To Marie the offer was as disturbing as it was perplexing. For a long time she lived under the fear that despite Sergei's rejection of the offer, the government might still take the children away. The very thought of such a development left Marie morally and physically enervated, and her health shaken. In August, 1844, Marie asked St. Petersburg for permission to reside in Irkutsk until her health was improved. The request was granted for her and her children, not for her husband. She could not leave a sick husband behind and, she believed, it would be difficult for her to recover her health while living alone. The government yielded only half way: Sergei was allowed to visit her in Irkutsk occasionally "with the permission of the governor."

In 1844 Marie learned that her mother had died in Rome. Shortly afterwards she received the news that her brother Nikita had died. The chain of sorrowful tidings stunned Marie particularly, because she had contemplated that her mother might take charge of her son's education. Now she had no choice but to apply once more for admission of the boy to the Irkutsk gymnasium. To her pleasant surprise, Governor Rupert supported the application, for he reasoned that such an education "would give the youth direction that would harmonize with the view of the government." The issue of dropping the boy's family name was not raised. He duly entered the fifth class of the gymnasium, and in 1849 graduated with a gold medal.

Upon graduation Mikhail was unable to enter the university, because the government thought it wiser to have him enter government service, where it could watch over his career. General N. N. Muraviev, who had become recently governor of Eastern Siberia, included him in his administration. Muraviev believed that the young man deserved special attention "since his conduct and application were exceptional and acceptable due to his upbringing at the home of his parents." Here was once again proof of the milder climate of Muraviev's administration in dealing with the families of the Decembrists. The former rigid rules yielded to more rational solutions of some daily difficulties.

In 1850 Marie's sister Sophie was granted permission to visit the Volkonskys in Irkutsk and she spent several weeks with them. It was the first time in nearly a quarter of a century that a relative from western Russia had been permitted to visit the exiles in Siberia. The only condition attached to the permission had been the demand that she pledge not to take any letters or to enter into any correspondence with exiles whom she might meet in Siberia.

Another happy omen was that the Volkonsky's daughter, Elena, after marrying an official employed in the office of the governor, was able to depart with her husband for St. Petersburg. As no one challenged the right of Elena, the Siberian-born daughter of an exiled "state criminal," to reside in the capital, an air of spring permeated the entire situation.

Unfortunately Marie's health was declining rapidly in the severe climate. Her request to the government to go to Moscow for medical consultation was denied on the ground "that there was no precedence that wives of exiles who joined their husbands could return as long as their husbands remained in Siberia." But on this occasion the Empress came to the defense of Marie, and in August, 1855, the desired permit was granted. Marie went to Moscow, where she resided with her daughter, while Sergei Volkonsky, himself seriously ill, remained in Siberia alone. A little over a year later, the long-awaited amnesty allowing the Decembrists to return to western Russia was proclaimed, and Sergei, in full haste, hurried westward to join his wife.

As soon as Volkonsky had been informed of the amnesty he gathered his few meager belongings, and rushed "home." A month later he was in the arms of his friends and relatives. After a span of over three decades Volkonsky and his family met in Moscow, but he was forbidden to reside there. He was assigned to live in the southern village of Voronki, in the province of Chernigov.

Volkonsky's return west was a happy occasion, though seriously marred by the state of his own health as well as the health of his wife. Marie was urged to go abroad for medical treatment and Volkonsky received permission to visit her. But so precarious was his condition in view of the cumulative effects of exile and medical neglect, that he was forced to discontinue his journey when he reached Dresden. His permit for a three-month absence from his homeland was extended for another three months.

Meanwhile Marie's illness, diagnosed by doctors as an inflammation of the liver, continued to get worse. Long years in exile reduced her resistance, and neither medicine nor mineral baths could relieve the agonizing pain she suffered. She returned to Voronki where on August 10, 1865, she died at the age of fifty-six. Her bed-ridden husband was not able to rush to her side even for the funeral. Shortly afterwards he had a stroke and was confined to a wheel chair. Mentally alert, he tried to write his memoirs, but on November 28, 1865, he died suddenly, while in the middle of a sentence. "The Emperor said to me: 'I . . . .'" were the last words he wrote.

Sergei was buried in the village of Voronki, side by side with Marie. At last they were together again, and in eternal peace.

6

Two French Brides

Camilla Ledantu

The title of Nekrasov's poem, "Russian Women," requires correction. Two of the women who followed the
Decembrists into exile were French. Nekrasov had planned
to write a longer poem, entitled, "The Decembrist Wives,"
but never completed it. He called his poem "Russian
Women," because he dealt only with Katasha and Marie.[1]
But the story of the French brides who followed the men
they loved to Siberia deserves to be told.

It was fashionable during the nineteenth century to
have private tutors in the homes of "respectable" families.
Since 1789 there had been an increasing flow of emigrés
from France to Russia. Many of them landed as tutors in
the homes of the Decembrists, as illustrated in the case of
the Decembrist Vasilii Ivashev.

The Ivashev family of the Simbirsk province consisted
of General Peter Ivashev, his wife, and five children. One

[1] See, for instance, the evaluation of Nekrasov's poem by Prince D. S. Mirsky, *A
History of Russian Literature From the Earliest Times to the Death of Dostoyevsky,
1881.* (New York, Knopf, 1934), pp. 300-302.

of the boys, Vasilii, destined to be a Decembrist, was entrusted in his youth to a French tutor Mr. Dinocours, while
the daughters were trained by two governesses, Mme de
Sancy and Mme Ledantu. The Ivashev household spent
usually the winters either in Moscow or in St. Petersburg.

Mme Ledantu had herself three daughters. One of them
eventually married a prominent landlord, V. Grigorovich.
Their son, D. V. Grigorovich, was to become a well-known
writer. Her daughter Camilla Petrovna met a young man,
Vasili Ivashev, who was groomed for a military career. Of
noble birth and great wealth, Vasili spent his leaves at
his home where he came to know Camilla well. The two
young people became friendly, though there was no indi-
cation of any love affair. Vasili derived much pleasure from
hearing Camilla's polished French; she enjoyed the company of the dashing young officer with a promising career.[2]

The summer visits of Vasili were discreetly and impatiently expected by Camilla, who at the time lived near the
estate with his married sister, Yazykova. In due course
Camilla came to revere the cultured army officer, though
she never revealed any sentiments of the heart, nor would
she dare to speak about it, considering her social status.

Vasili served in the Second Army located in the south,
where a secret society was formed, known as the "Southern Society." In 1820 Vasili joined the organization to
which many of his friends and acquaintances belonged,
including such figures as P. I. Pestel. Vasili soon became
an active member, prominent to the extent that he was
elected as one of the six "boyars." Yet as months went by
and political difficulties mounted, Vasili retreated from
active participation. Still, secret reports to the authorities
state of the clandestine activities and the involvement of

[2] See N. I. Grech, *Zapiski o moyei zhizni* (Moscow, 1930), 515-516. See also Memories of the grand-daughter of V. Ivashev, O. K. Bulanova, *Roman dekabrista. Dekabrist
V. P. Ivashev i ego semya* (Moscow, 1925).

Vasili. However, nothing happened to him until the events of December 14/26, 1825 in St. Petersburg.

Camilla had some suspicions of Vasili's association with clandestine organizations, but she had no notion of the nature of the society, nor was she aware of the consequences discovery might entail. When the storm suddenly broke and Vasili found himself detained, the two did not have time to gather their wits and discuss the future.

Following the arrest of Pestel, Vasili was sent north and placed in the Peter and Paul fortress, totally isolated and unable to communicate with anyone. Separation could not erase Camilla's memories or sentiments. She was horrified by the very thought of what might happen to Vasili and shared her trepidations with her mother who in desperation consulted Mme de Sancy. Being never strong or of robust health, Camilla was now physically and morally exhausted. By nature uncommunicative, Camilla became increasingly secretive, and suffered fits of depression.

After having conferred with Mme de Sancy, Mme Ledantu decided that Camilla must return to Moscow and be taken to the countryside for a thorough rest. She did so, but the health of Camilla continued to deteriorate and her thoughts wandered far away from maternal care. Camilla revealed none of her thoughts and kept getting worse, while her mother in desperation tried to locate desirable suitors. It was all in vain, for her daughter remained totally indifferent to all pleas or marital schemes.

While in this state, Camilla learned about Annenkov, the Decembrist who in exile married the French girl Pauline Gueble, and she began to scheme to do likewise, but long was unable to muster enough courage to open her heart to anyone. Finally, one day Camilla revealed to her mother that she thought of doing what Mlle Gueble had done—to share her future with the man with whom she had been in love secretly. After long hesitance and much tear shedding, the mother agreed to let her follow Vasili to Siberia "if such sacrifice would restore her health."[3]

For weeks Camilla was bed-ridden. Her mother finally gathered enough courage to sit down and write a letter to Mme Ivasheva, the mother of Vasili. The essence of the message was that Camilla, in all sincerity, was ready "to share the chain weight of exile" and marry Vasili. She therefore wished to ask the consent of the Ivashev family. After much thought Mme Ivasheva replied that the family was prepared "with open arms to receive Camilla for her noble readiness to share the heavy sacrifices of their son." Before replying, however, Mme Ivasheva had dispatched the letter to her son in Siberia for his opinion. There followed a long tale of parental discussion and search for governmental permission.[4]

Meanwhile Vasili, whose career had come to an abrupt end, was resentful, bitter, and rebellious in exile. He could not reconcile himself to the turn of events. He tried to occupy himself by painting portraits; he tried to write. But his rebellious nature would not permit him to resign himself to such pursuits. He began to contemplate escaping to China.[5] Two of his close friends to whom he revealed his plan, argued him out of it. They urged him to stay and to wait for other opportunities. After discussing *le pour et le contre* of the entire plot, Ivashev was convinced that it would be total folly, and he abandoned the scheme.

It was in the midst of such plotting that Vasili was suddenly summoned to the commandant and asked whether he would be willing for Camilla to join him in Siberia for the purpose of marriage. Vasili fully recognized the sacrifices Camilla would have to make in marrying a "state

[3] A. M. Venevitinov, "Roman dekabrista," *Russakaya mysl'*, X, 1885, 123-124.
[4] A. Belyayev, *Vospominaniya dekabrista o perezhitom i perechuvstvovannom*, ed. by A. S. Suvorin (St. Petersburg, 1882), particularly pp. 216-219.
[5] Venevitinov, "Roman dekabrista," 128-129.

criminal" in Siberia. After much agonizing contemplation, he hesitatingly consented, cognizant of the grave responsibility undertaken and of the obligations involved. His friends promised to render him all necessary assistance and were delighted that this would end Vasili's dreams of escape to China.

After Mme Ivasheva formally agreed to her son's marriage, Camilla dispatched a touching message to her future mother-in-law. Among other things, Camilla, with unusual humility, said:

> . . . I must confess, I do not deserve your praise, for I am not always certain that I am capable of delivering the solace to your son. Finally, what is then the essence of my merit? I do not offer sacrifice by rejecting the world which does not attract me anyway. Only my family which is dear to me I must leave. For four years my family suffered because my incomprehensible secretiveness baffled them . . . . Love me as I love you, love me as a mother who permits me to dedicate my life to her dear son. My entire virtue is that I love Vasili and I limit my aspiration to a particle of the love, which his parents may render me.[6]

Henceforth Camilla always ended her letters to the Ivashevs as "your devoted daughter."

Nicholas I gave his personal consent to the marriage. "If her parents as well as the Ivashevs agree, I on my part am unable to oppose."

The winter of 1829-1830 arrived and it was too late to make the journey east. The Ivashevs hoped to have Camilla spend the time with them in Moscow, but a cholera epidemic and the set-up quarantines prevented her from entering the city. It was only in the spring that Camilla was finally able to start her long eastward journey.

Meanwhile in July 1830 all the prisoners began their exodus from Chita to Petrovsk. The long journey and

[6] *Ibid.*, 135-136.

settlement were not completed until the fall. Camilla reached Petrovsk only in 1831, a year after Vasili had learned of her decision to join him. Five days later they were married and Commandant Leparsky offered to the newlyweds his quarters for the first few days. Eventually Camilla moved into her own house and became a full fledged member of the "Ladies' Club."

The marriage ceremony was unusual, to say the least. Due to the kindness of the good Commandant Leparsky, the men did not have to wear the leg chains, and although the guards accompanied the bridegroom, they did not bear arms. The marriage ceremony was not marred by the instructions that had prevailed at the time of the wedding of the other French bride to be discussed below.[7]

The Ivashevs did not have a happy family life either at Petrovsk or at Turinsk, where they moved at the end of 1835. Their first child died at the age of two. In 1839 Camilla, who was eight months pregnant, caught a severe cold. Complications followed due to the usual lack of medical attention, and she died in December of the same year at the age of thirty-five. "You will share the tragedy with poor Ivashev," I. I. Pushchin wrote to Obolensky. "On December 30 he lost his good wife and you can imagine what a cruel blow it delivered to all of us. It is difficult to get accustomed to the thought that Camilla is no more with us. Peacefully she consoled her husband, blessed the children, said farewell to her friends . . . . We are all orphans without her, and this premature loss arouses resentment in our hearts . . . ."[8]

---

[7] See O. K. Bulanova, *Roman dekabrista, Dekabrist V. P. Ivashev i ego vremya.* I. D. Yakushkin presents a different version of the marriage, stripping it of all romantic embellishments. Yakushkin believed that Camilla was more interested in Ivashev's wealth and motivated more by his social status than sentimental notions. See Yakushkin, *Zapiski, stat'i, pis'ma dekabrista,* 172-76.

[8] I. I. Pushchin, *Zapiski dekabrista* (Moscow, 1927), 128.

Vasili was left with three children—Marie, Piotr, and Vera—six, four, and two years old respectively. Heart-broken, dazed, and lonely, he died of apoplexy on the eve of the first anniversary of Camilla's death, on December 28, 1840. The upbringing and education of the orphaned children was entrusted eventually to his sister, Princess E. P. Khovanskaya. The amnesty of 1856 restored to them their hereditary ranks.

Pauline Geueble

We know more about the life and feelings of the other French bride, Pauline (Pelageya Yegorovna) Annenkova, née Geueble, because she lived longer and left behind fairly informative memoirs.[9] Pauline Geueble came from Nancy, France. Her father, a French army officer, was killed by the Spanish guerrillas during the Napoleonic wars. In Russia Pauline represented a French firm of fashions. Here she met the attractive looking, socially prominent, and wealthy young lieutenant of the Cavalry Guard, Ivan A. Annenkov.

Pauline was witty, dynamic, practical and resourceful, full of whim, yet rational whenever occasion demanded. She was a fastidious cook, a quality that was to prove particularly helpful in the dreary years of exile. She had considerable musical talent, a pleasing contralto, and sang well; she often entertained friends and guests in exile and upon her return from exile at home.

Annenkov and Pauline Geueble fell in love and soon began to contemplate marriage. Annenkov's mother was in total charge of the estate. She was an egotistical, self-centered, capricious, and exceedingly temperamental

[9]Pauline Y. Annenkova, *Zapiski, zheny dekabrista* (Petrograd: "Promotei," n.d.). A later edition includes also reminiscences of Pauline's daughter and other material, including a preface and notations by S. Gessen and D. Predtechensky. See *Vospominaniya Poliny Annenkovoi*, second edition (Moscow, Izdatel'stvo Politkatorzhan, 1932).

woman, whose attitude had a dampening effect upon the romantic ardor of both lovers. Pauline had particular misgivings and did not wish to irritate the petulant lady whose good will might be of vital concern in her future life.[10]

Ivan A. Annenkov, as the son of a prominent nobleman and landlord, was educated by two tutors at home, one Swiss and the other French; later he attended the University of Moscow, though he did not graduate, since he chose a military career. His father, a retired captain of the famous Lifeguard Preobrazhensky Regiment, played a leading role in the ranks of the nobility of Nizhnii Novgorod. His mother, Anne, was the daughter of the Governor General of Irkutsk, Ivan V. Jakoby. In 1820 Ivan Annenkov, in a hasty challenge to a duel over some trifling matter, killed his friend V. Ya. Lanskoy. Three years later his only brother Gregory was killed in a duel. The two episodes left a profound impression upon Ivan for the rest of his life.

Though Ivan favored marriage, Pauline, with Gallic rationality, advised to act with caution and not to antagonize his mother. She coolly reasoned that since Ivan was prominent and wealthy and she was a poor, hardworking girl, barely making a living, it would be better for all concerned that sufficient time be allowed to think things over. Hasty action, she feared, might lead the ill-tempered woman to disinherit her son. Logically and fairly Pauline figured that she had no right to ruin Ivan's future, nor break up his family.[11] Things became more involved when Pauline became pregnant and in April 1826 gave birth to a girl. It took much courage in those days to admit later to the authorities that Pauline Geueble, the bride of Ivan Annenkov, was already the mother of his child.

[10] See *Russkaya starina*, XXXII, 1888, 405.

[11] Annenkova, *Zapiski*, 30, 31, new edition, 68, 69.

The Decembrist revolt changed the entire situation overnight. The former army officer, with his once bright future, was suddenly a state criminal, sentenced to years of hard labor and to subsequent exile in Siberia.

But Pauline remained loyal to her lover. She pledged to join Ivan no matter where fate might cast him. While Ivan was in prison, Pauline, after giving birth to their daughter, born out of wedlock, lay bedridden for nearly three months with a lingering illness. Slow in recovering, she did not let her weakness intervene with her determination to follow her man to the remotest corner of the earth. As she repeatedly counselled herself, "If you dare, you will succeed!"[12]

In one of her pleas Pauline wrote:

> Je renonce à ma patrie et remplirai pieusement tout ce que les lois me prescriront. Annenkoff m'avait promis l'hymenée. N'ayant pu accomplir sa promesse, je ne doute pas cependant, qu'il ne persiste dans le même sentiment. Sa majesté n'a qu'à l'ordonner, j'attendrais avec la plus grande resignation.[13]

Pauline was a Roman Catholic, but the father of her child was of Russian Orthodox faith. After some hesitation and conflicting advice, Pauline had the baby girl baptized in the Orthodox faith. She made arrangements to leave the baby with a reliable, elderly lady she knew in Moscow, a certain Mme Charpantié, as children were barred from accompanying their parents into exile.

Ivan was sentenced to twenty years of hard labor and the term was later cut in half, followed by exile. The sentence did not discourage Pauline, despite the fact that many people from the Emperor down tried to talk her out of going to Siberia. She was warned that if she went, she

[12] *Russkaya starina*, IX, 1885, 116-142.
[13] Annenkova, *Zapiski*, 84, new edition, 123.

would find herself in a totally alien country, a completely unknown environment, and would be forced to reside amidst a people whose language she was unable to speak or have difficulty to learn. But Pauline remained faithful to her virtuous resolve. It was a gallantry rare in history.[14]

Pauline appealed directly to Nicholas I to grant her permission to follow Ivan Annenkov, "one of the state criminals so that she would be able to marry him in exile, join him, share his fate, and never part from him." Nicholas I frigidly reminded her that Siberia was not the kind of country where she might find happiness, but since she insisted despite of sufficient warnings, he was inclined to grant his consent. The treasured permission was received in November, 1827, and Pauline left Moscow on her adventurous journey eastward, on the frosty morning of December 23.[15]

Pauline passed Kazan in early January. She reached the city of Ekaterinburg (now Sverdlovsk) three weeks later. From here she proceeded to Tomsk and finally to Irkutsk, where she arrived nearly frost-bitten. Officials were reluctant to allow her to proceed further, but after a brief delay, Pauline managed to overcome their objections. She reached Chita in mid-March, after two and a half months of gruelling travel by horse-drawn vehicles.[16]

In Chita Pauline met Natalya F. Fonvizina, Alexandra I. Davydova, Alexandra Muravieva, and later Anna V. Rosen, who had special difficulties in obtaining permission to come to Siberia. Katasha Trubetskaya and Marie Volkonskaya also were in town. These women quickly formed the nucleus of the feminine group that constituted the bulwark of the Decembrist colony. They nourished the moral

---

[14] *Ibid.*, 55, new edition, 98.
[15] *Russkaya starina*, III, 1901, 673-674.
[16] Annenkova, *Zapiski*, 93-94; 108-109; new edition, 142-144; 151-152.

strength of the men and acted as champions of their interests, be it to obtain windows in their Nerchinsk prison cells or to bridle the overbearing conduct of a boorish official such as the head of the Nerchinsk mines, T. V. Burnashev.

From the day of her departure for Siberia throughout the years of exile, Pauline was to share the burden of guilt and punishment imposed on the man she loved. Like the other Decembrist wives, she had to manage on an officially prescribed meager monthly allowance and on frequent occasions had to deny herself essential food in order to share meals with her husband. Yet Pauline was in particularly difficult straits. The shortages in food, clothing, and medical supplies she experienced and the general hardships of life she encountered in Siberia (which Count K. V. Nesselrode once called "the bottom of the sack"), may be gleaned from the fact that she gave birth to eighteen children, of whom only six survived.

Commandant Leparsky introduced Pauline to the daily routine of life in exile. The women were forbidden to communicate with the prisoners; they could not attend public entertainments; they could not take alcoholic beverages to the prison. Pauline had to keep the prison authorities informed of her place of residence at all times. She could visit Ivan only at times specifically designated by the authorities. All her letters, whether to friends in western Russia or abroad had to be sent through administrative channels and censored. She had to keep a record of all monthly allowances and disbursements, and balance them accurately. All this and the requirement that she converse with Ivan exclusively in Russian were particularly trying for Pauline, whose knowledge of the language was extremely limited.

Ivan and Pauline were married in the local Nerchinsk

chapel. Commandant Leparsky acted as the nuptial godfather, while Mme Fonvizina, a fellow exile, acted as the nuptial godmother. Leparsky and Pauline both were Roman Catholics and not familiar with the Orthodox ritual. The wedding ceremony was the more perfunctory as no singers were to be found for the occasion. Before the bridegroom entered the chapel his leg chains were removed, but they were put back again shortly after the ceremony and prison life assumed its normal course for him.

In December 1835 Ivan completed his term of penal servitude and was sent into exile to the village of Bel'skoye (Irkutsk province), and three years later, moved to Turinsk (Tobolsk province). After the appeal of Mme Annenkova, Ivan was permitted to join the civil service in Siberia. Gradually advancing, he became assessor of the Tobolsk Public Charity Board, in which capacity he served until 1856, when the amnesty manifesto permitted him to return to western Russia, where he was an active leader of the nobility in his province (Nizhni-Novgorod). Pauline died in September 1876; Ivan a year and a half later, in January 1878.

Epilogue

It would be repetitious to continue in detail with the sorrowful story of the wives of the Decembrists. With few exceptions, the tragedy affected them all with equal force and compelled them to subordinate themselves within the same or nearby location in a similar dull, provincial atmosphere. What adjustments it must have taken to be transplanted from the glittering capital to a village in "the bottom of the sack"!

Aside from serving as pillars of moral assistance to their husbands, the Decembrist wives occupied themselves by managing their modest homes.

With the arrival of the spring season, they cultivated small plots near their houses. They planted vegetables, fruit trees, and whatever greenery the soil and climate favored. The women occupied themselves also with various domestic chores, preparing meals, patching old clothes, or embroidering blouses. One task the aristocratic ladies abhorred was the killing of fowl. They envied Pauline for her skill and "professional composure" in performing the task.

During the long winter nights the women gathered at each other's homes to sew, read, and discuss various subjects. By some tacit consent they never touched upon the subject that had led their men into exile. By sharing the deprivations, hard labor, and tribulations of daily life they gained strength and composure in unity and found moments of joy as well as sorrow. "There was much poetry in our lives," recalled Pauline in her memoirs.

As a gesture of imperial kindness the prisoners were rewarded in the summer of 1828 for "good behavior" by being freed from wearing iron chains, though their hard labor sentences remained in effect. The physical effect of the hard labor was bound to be profound on most of them who had never before been engaged in manual labor. When Katasha first saw Annenkov, she could hardly recognize him. The man she had known as a dashing army officer and gallant dancer, now was a prematurely aged man, unshaven, in a worn overcoat held together around the waist with a piece of rope.

E. P. Naryshkina, the only daughter of Count P. Konovnitsyn, a prominent figure in St. Petersburg, had been barely twenty-three years of age when she had set out for Siberia in 1827 to follow her husband. When she found him in chains, upon meeting him for the first time, she fainted away.

Valorous, insouciant, and merry on the surface, Naryshkina began to brood in exile. The uncertain future in the dull and distant town of Chita and the confinement and the poor health of her husband undermined her valor. Not robust to begin with, she was weakened by frequent and severe colds. Confined to bed repeatedly, she kept wondering how long she could last.

In 1833 the Naryshkins were sent to Kurgan, in western Siberia. But Naryshkina was unable to shake off the illness that slowly kept sapping her health. The poet V. A. Zhukovsky, after meeting her at Kurgan, was deeply moved by her "noble simplicity, poise and valorous bearing of sorrow." He did not realize that her endurance was slowly but surely undermining her tender existence.

At the end of 1837 Naryshkin was sent to the Caucasus

as a common soldier. Service amidst the warlike natives was hazardous, and Naryshkina was in a continued state of agitation and deep concern over the fate of her husband. Her tired soul had little chance to find peace in the Caucasus. In 1844 Naryshkin was retired and ordered to reside permanently in a village near Tula. He died in 1867 and was buried in Moscow; his wife did not survive him by long and was buried next to him. Their only child was an adopted girl, Ulyana.

The story of Baroness Anna V. Rosen is another illustration of the tragic fate that had befallen the Decembrist wives. She arrived in Petrovsk in 1830. Two years later they were exiled to Kurgan (Tobolsk). Kurgan was a small town on the banks of the Tobol River, with a population of less than 2,000, a church, and something that resembled a school. A dull, typical frontier town, with wooden houses, where a monotonous existence prevailed except for the brief annual fair. Here the Rosens resided until the fall of 1837, when Baron Rosen was ordered to serve in the Caucasian army as a common soldier. Two years later he was discharged on account of ill health and was ordered to reside in Estonia, near Narva, on the estate of his brother. Here he lived until 1856, when the amnesty restored his freedom. He died in 1884.

The case of A. V. Yental'tsev, another Decembrist, and his wife was even sadder. After completing his prison term Yental'tsev and wife were exiled to Yalutorovsk (Tobolsk). The loneliness of this town had a deadly effect on both of them. Within a short time Yental'tsev began to show signs of mental illness. To live with a mentally disturbed man in Siberian exile was a dreadful prospect. Yental'tseva began to plead that she be granted permission to return with her husband to western Russia, but her appeals were denied. The agony of her fate lasted until 1845, when her husband died. She was granted a small pension which gave her no choice but to remain in Yalutorovsk. She remained a lonely soul in this distant land until 1856, when the amnesty enabled her to return to western Russia. Like her friends, she returned from exile a morally broken down, physically drained woman. Two years later she died in a land that seem alien, callous, and void of meaning.

All told, at the time of the amnesty, there were thirty-four survivors in exile. Of these thirteen resided in western, and twenty-one in eastern Siberia. Because of poor health, loss of ties with friends or kins, many of the Decembrists preferred to remain in Siberia. As one of them morosely commented when informed of the amnesty, "the grave in western Russia would not be warmer than in Siberia."[1]

From the standpoint of the nineteenth century, the Decembrist revolt was a transient nightmare in Russian history. An offshoot of youthful enthusiasm inspired from abroad, it was bound to end on Russian soil in a political fiasco. Viewed from a more distant perspective the actions of the Decembrists and the subsequent conduct of their wives, take on new significance. Their dramatic lives turn into a hymn.

The drama that unfolded on Senate Square in St. Petersburg in December 1825 assumed symbolic meaning of political inevitability, and of personal heroism. The conduct of the wives of the Decembrists acquired an aura of profound political and social martyrdom. Nicholas I aimed from the very beginning to isolate all the elements related to Decembrism; he endeavored to erase the entire nightmare. But the wives of the Decembrists unwittingly prevented the event from passing into oblivion. Their

[1] See B. G. Kubalov, "Dekabristy i amnistiya," 143-159.

lives perpetuated the memory of Decembrism and of the Decembrists, and created a legend of political martyrdom.[2]

Throughout his lifetime Nicholas I acidulously referred to the Decembrists as "My December friends," while his minister of education, Count S. S. Uvarov, repeatedly expressed his fear that Decembrism had not been totally uprooted.[3] Small wonder officialdom even after the magnanimous amnesty of 1856, kept most of the returned Decembrists under surveillance for most of their remaining years.

History shows that the seeds of revolution by the Decembrists took deeper root in the soil of Russia than contemporaries had realized. The wives of the Decembrists aided in nurturing the tender sprouts, unaware of the role they played in the historical process. Their example inspired other women of the nineteenth century— Sophia Perovskaya, Vera Figner, and Catherine Breshkovskaya, to name just a few—to engage in political activities and to challenge autocracy.

The unselfishness of the wives of the Decembrists evoked the highest praise. As A. P. Belyayev extolled:

> Honor and ornament of your sex! Fame of the land that produced you! Glory to the men who proved worthy of the love and devotion of such amazing, peerless women! Despite your youth, your tenderness and weakness of your sex, you became the perfect example of self-renounced valor and fortitude! May your names be immortal![4]

---

[2] M. N. Gernet, *Istoriya tsarskoy tyurmy* (Moscow, 1951), II, 195 .

[3] N. Barsukov, *Zhizn' i trudy M. L. Pogodina* (St. Petersburg, 1891), IV, 227.

[4] Cited by M. M. Khin, "Zheny dekabristov," 683.

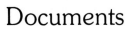

Documents

A

Instructions from Governor General A. S. Lavinsky to I. B. Zeidler, Governor of Irkutsk

[Nov. 1827   ?]

. . . Being aware of the fact that the wives of the convicts are unable to follow their husbands to Nerchinsk, though some may get as far as Irkutsk, I place upon you the duty to stop them at that city and see that they return to Russia.

You are to make the following clear to them:

1) If they follow their husbands and continue conjugal relations, they must, naturally, share their fate and lose their former status, that is, they will be recognized only as wives of exiled hard labor convicts, while the children they may bear in Siberia will become industrial peasants [*possessionnye krestyane*].

2) As soon as the women set out for the Nerchinsk region they should be informed that they are not permitted to take any money or valuables with them. This is mainly because it is forbidden by present regulations and necessary also for personal safety. Former criminals roaming the country are liable to attack persons in possession of money or valuable articles.

3) With their departure for Nerchinsk, they lose their rights

to own serfs; this applies to the serfs who accompany them.

At the same time it is necessary to tell these people that transportation in the fall months across Lake Baikal is extremely hazardous and even impossible. They are to be warned of the shortage of state transport boats or of the difficulty of con-tracting such boats from private dealers. To persuade them successfully, Your Excellency, try to change their views in private discussions which will undoubtedly be held at your private residence.

If, however, after accurately carrying out these instructions you find they still insist upon pursuing their goal, do not hinder their exit from Irkutsk to Nerchinsk. In that case, entirely change your tone in dealing with them. Assume the attitude of an official who deals with wives of hard-labor prisoners; assume the appropriate tone of a high official who is fulfilling his duties. In fact, carry out what has been said above; at first warn them and render wise counsel, namely:

(a) Seal all the money which they possess, all valuable items and so on, according to the description they cite, and after reporting and obtaining a personal signature of the owner, that it is taken away from them, deposit it with the Irkutsk provincial treasury. To eliminate all suspicions, this measure must be enacted by a special commission made up of one or two mem-bers of the Chief Administration, the chairman of the local administration, the attorney general, all of them under your chairmanship. Travel expenses are to be issued to them from their own funds.

(b) Of the serfs who have come with them, allow one serf per person to follow, but only those serfs who will volunteer, proving their consent either by personal signature or, in case of illiteracy, in a statement notarized by the local administration. The rest may be invited to return to Russia after the proper papers are issued to them.

Having shown, on my part, the means, based on legitimate regulations that must serve as a guide to conduct in this matter, and expecting, Your Excellency, explicit execution of these, I hope that you and your personal participation will not neglect all possible means to attain the aim to disuade the wives of the criminals from carrying on their intentions, emanating from ignorance of local Siberian conditions and the regulations that are in effect in that country. If, however, all your efforts prove futile, then, Your Excellency, act in accordance with these directions, but inform me immediately concerning all the circumstances related to these women, and the general means you will adopt.

Finally, in case any one has already passed Irkutsk before this instruction reaches you, I beg Your Excellency to assume the task of personally seeing to it that such a person be returned to the city where proper authorities may be found or stop such persons in Verkhneudinsk, for escape of a single person may inspire others to similar rights to proceed to Nerchinsk.[1]

[1] V. Pokrovsky, *Zheny dekabristov*, 2-3; "Iz proshlogo. K istorii dekabristov," *Isto-richesky vestnik*, V, 1898, 675-77.

B

A Letter from M. N. Volkonskaya to her Husband, S. G. Volkonsky

June 28, 1826

I just received your letter, my dear. Mixed feelings of happiness and bitterness. Do not blame yourself, my poor Sergei, that you have forever wrecked my happiness. This will never happen as long as you will retain your sense of loyalty and faith and as long as I will have a glimmer of hope that we will be together with our dear child. I kissed dear Nikolenka a thousand times and gave him your letter, which he played with and held up to his mouth, as he does with everything he gets hold of. It was touching to watch him: it seemed as if he wanted to kiss it.

My brothers thank you for everything you asked me to pass on. They are keenly interested in your fate and presently incapable to hold anything against you at this time of misfortune. I passed your gratitude to Countess Branitskaya and she seemed to have been touched by it. Sophie kisses you and asks me to pass to you many, many of her best wishes. We often talk about you.

Do not think, my dear, that I allow myself to go into depression. Your exemplary behavior supports me, while my son reminds me of my duties. I am convinced of the sympathies of the kind Princess Repnina. How I love her, marvel at her and wish that you might have the pleasure of solace to see your superb sister. I am convinced that she will do everything with the hope that it will alleviate your lot. You write that I agree with her way of thinking. This does not surprise me. We always think of you and since we both know your character our opinion about you must coincide. The thought that you may see your wonderful sister who is worthy of respect, and your marvellous niece, cheers me. Oh, how happy you would be to see your son! Do not resent our arrival in Petersburg. As soon as his teeth are cut there will be no danger.

Good bye, my dear. Always retain your submission to Providence, think of your son. I do not write about your god-child Julie since Ivan Maksimov is at the Repnins.[2]

---

[2] *Pamyati dekabristov. Sbornik materialov* (Leningrad, 1926), II, 94-95.

C

From Governor I. B. Zeidler to Princess Ekaterina Ivanovna Trubetskaya

January 19, 1827
Irkutsk

Dear Madame,

Princess Ekaterina Ivanovna!

I received your letter, informing me that you, for reasons explained, are unable to abandon your intention to follow your husband and request that you be allowed to go with him. Having presented to you all the difficulties and disadvantages of your newly assumed position and noting your firm intentions, I can no more stop you. Still, I consider it my duty to repeat to you in written form, that by following your husband and continuing your matrimonial relations with him, you naturally become involved in his fate: you lose your former rank while your children born in Siberia will become state peasants [*kazionnye krestyane*].

Secondly, you will not be allowed to carry with you either money or valuable items.

Thirdly, with your departure for Nerchinsk there will be annulled your rights to own the serfs who came with you; only one is permitted to follow you voluntarily. If you still remain firm in your intention, and to avoid any misunderstanding, you must record all valuable items and money with the Commission made up of several members; you are requested that you present to the same Commission, the entire amount of money in your possession, gold, silver or valuable items. The same Commission will also have the duty to leave for your use, such things as clothes and other necessary things not considered as valuable items. All other things will properly be recorded in your presence, certified by your personal signature, and then deposited in sealed form with the circuit treasury. An itemized copy will be handed to you for your information. I have the honor to inform you that this is to be executed on this date at 11:00 A.M.

I remain sincerely yours,
Dear Madame,
Your obedient servant,
Ivan Zeidler[3]

---

[3] S. P. Trubetskoy, *Zapiski* (St. Petersburg, 1907), 116-117.

D

Letter from Marie Volkonskaya to her Mother-in-Law

Chita
September 26, 1827

Here I am in Chita, my tenderly loved Maman, after a very tiring trip. I travelled without a maid, along terrible roads together with Katen'ka [Katasha]. The cold in the mountains caused terrible suffering. My husband and his fellow travellers are still on the road, and I am waiting for him with inexplicable anxiety: he spat blood on the day of my departure. I fear terribly that travel will tire him. Local post travel is even more uncomfortable than Russian travel and it will badly affect his poor lungs.

I found Mmes Naryshkina, Yental'tseva, and Muravieva subjected to the identical regulations which were prescribed to us in Blagodatsk. It means that for a long time I will be able to see my husband only twice a week. My Lord, when will the trials end for me and for poor Sergei, whose health demands all my attention. How many times did I wish to ask my mother-in-law that she assist me to obtain permission to see him daily.

The women have formed here some kind of a family. They accept each other with open arms—how misfortune brings people together! Mme Yental'tseva brought me the toys of my poor little boy, who was able to pronounce my name and the name of his father. I was very touched by the attention of this wonderful woman. We live together and she is our economist who teaches me frugality. My living quarters are far more comfortable than the one in Blagodatsk; at least here I have a place for a table to write, an embroidering frame and the clavichord.

Yesterday I received a letter from father which did me much good. Dear Daddy, I am thankful to you for the boundless tenderness which you always have shown me. I kiss your hands and feet a million times.

I thank my dear sisters for their letters and leave you, my adorable mother, for I am in a total state of exhaustion. I do not understand even what I am writing, for the women around me make so much noise. Again, good-bye, from the depth of my heart. I kiss your hands.

Your daughter,
Marie Volkonskaya

Do not forget to send me my fur-trimmed jacket [*katsaveika*] and gown that are in Bolty [the Volkonsky estate in the province of Kiev].[4]

---

[4] *Letopisi. Dekabristy* (Moscow, 1938), book III, 89-90.

E

Excerpt from a Letter of Marie Volkonskaya to Her Mother

November 14, 1827

I must inform you, dear Maman, that from the time of my departure from Petersburg, I had only the money I took with me [700 rubles], and in addition one thousand rubles which I received from my father. Travel, the sending back of the men [who accompanied Marie], and our trip from Blagodatsk led to unforeseen expenses, the result of which is that I find myself at present in a difficult situation. I have long ago warned my brother Repnin[5] about this, but either my letter has not reached him, or he thinks that I took advantage of the letter of credit, which Feodor, the cook, was to bring me, but because of his death, I did not get. Since you are, dear Maman, so kind as to send me to the account of my wardship the annual supply of all kinds of provisions from the Makarev fair, I ask food supplies only. But Sergei needs woolen clothes, linen, and lots of tobacco. All these things are most unavailable here or are too expensive for us, considering the allowance they issue us . . . .

Your obedient daughter

Marie Volkonskaya

[5] N. G. Repnin, brother of Sergei Volkonsky, had inherited in 1801 the name of his grandfather on his mother's side, Fieldmarshal N. V. Repnin.

108

Sergei asks you to send him Fisher's *Entomology* or the *Science of Insects,* two volumes.[6]

[6] *Russkie propilei* (Moscow, 1915), I, 45-46.

F

Excerpt from a Letter of Marie Volkonskaya to Her Sister

Chita Prison
December 20, 1827

What can be said about our gloomy Siberia? Because of the frightfully low temperature I seldom see my friends, A. G. Muravieva, E. P. Naryshkina, N. D. Fonvizina, Pauline Annenkova and A. I. Davydova, surely less than I would like to. With Katya [Katasha Trubetskaya] and Mme Yental'tseva we are always together, since we manage a common household. We take turn cooking. The Lord has just created us for our prison situation and we get accustomed perfectly to each other. As I never see the dark side of things, I feel myself unfortunate only at times when Sergei becomes ill. If they would only allow me to share with him the cell and devote my life to him. I would consider myself a fortunate woman.

Your sister
Marie Volkonskaya[7]

[7] *Russkie propilei* (Moscow, 1915), I, 50-51.

G

Excerpt from a Letter of Marie Volkonskaya to Her Sister-in-Law, Zinaida

December 27, 1827
Chita Prison

One thing that distressed me in this letter [from Alina] was the epithet "poor," which your niece applies to me. I can assure you, my dear sister, this term is not at all a suitable one: I am perfectly fortunate that I find myself near Sergei. I pride myself that I belong to him. He is an example of subserviency and firmness. His health is again good, he diligently goes to work, which proves best of all that his strength has been restored. As to myself, I got used to my condition, I lead an active and preoccupied life. I find that there is nothing better than working with your hands. Such labor lulls your mind and there is no time for tormenting thoughts, while reading leads you to memories of the past.

I receive regularly letters from Maman and heartily am thankful to her for sending us provisions. Amidst the provisions that have arrived I am very happy to find bouillon, which enables me to make soup for Sergei, though not successfully since I am unable to find any ingredients. Katya is more skillful than

111

I am, but, on the other hand, none of my friends is able to repair or sew underwear as I do. With the coming of spring I will instruct them how to cultivate a garden. Here is how I discovered my many talents since we became separated. It is more than a year that I have left Nikolenka [the son], who is forever deprived of his father's blessings. Lord, if I were only able to live with both of them no matter where in Siberia!

The last few days the weather has been less cold: now it is only 25-30° [Fahr.] below. Think how it is to live in a country where you find such temperature to be very mild! I have renewed my hikes within the village limits since I am forbidden, without special permission, to walk beyond the limits.

What else can I tell you, my dear sister? Our life here is quiet and monotonous. We see our husbands twice weekly for three hours and are permitted to send them dinners. Often their clanking chains we hear make us run to the window whence, with bitter joy, we watch them go to work. They work five hours daily in two shifts, but their work is not excessive and good for them, because it allows them exercise.

Your sister
Marie Volkonskaya[8]

---

[8] *Russkie propilei* (Moscow, 1915), I, 53-54.

H

Letter from A. Lavinsky to
Count [Ivan Ivanovich] Dibich

No. 24
February 4, 1828
Irkutsk

Your Excellency,
  Dear Sir!
  Recently a seamstress arrived in Irkutsk, a French subject, Jeanette Paul [Pauline Gueble], accompanied by two serfs who belong to the Lady-in-Waiting Annenkova. She presented the passport enclosed herewith, issued to her by the Moscow Chief of Police last December for her journey to Nerchinsk, as well as an order of the Moscow Civil Governor for post horses. With her are also Andrei Matveev and Stefan Novikov, the two serfs, sent to accompany her to Irkutsk and then to be returned to Moscow.
  When I received from the police a report of their coming here and wishing to know the real reason for this foreign subject coming to Nerchinsk, I ordered to enquire from her personally the reasons. I have found that she came to marry a state criminal, Annenkov, and that the marriage was permitted by the authorities. However, she had not presented any evi-

113

dence with the exception of copies of her own letters to the Moscow Chief of Police. These were not certified either by the Governor of Moscow nor do these define the status of state criminals.

Having no information that this foreign lady be given the right to proceed to Chita where the state criminal is confined, I did not consider it within my right to issue her a permit to depart from Irkutsk. I will write beforehand to the Commandant of the Nerchinsk mines, General Leparsky, requesting information whether he received any such information concerning the above-mentioned person.

In case General Leparsky will ascertain that arrival in Chita is permitted, I will immediately allow her to depart from Irkutsk. If, however, General Leparsky has no such information about her, it will be my duty to obtain clarification from Your Excellency as to what I should do with this foreign lady. Until I get your reply I will not permit her to leave Irkutsk.

> With highest respect and devotion,
> I have the honor etc.
> (signed) A. Lavinsky[9]

---

[9] P. Y. Annenkova, *Zapiski zheny dekabrista* (Petrograd, n.d.), 157-158.

I

Excerpt from a Letter of Marie Volkonskaya to Her Mother-in-Law

January 12, 1829
Chita

. . . Forgive me, dear Maman, that I have annoyed you several times in my previous letters, concerning the retention of my pension . . . . A more weighty justification for this is that in the country where we live, people avoid us; it is unbelievable how they fear to associate with us, refuse to loan us most petty items, while my friends do not always have money either . . . .

Your subservient daughter,
Marie Volkonskaya[10]

---

[10] *Russkie propilei*, I, 58.

J

Excerpt from a Letter of Marie Volkonskaya to her Mother-in-Law

Chita
January 19, 1829

Three days ago was the dreadful anniversary [the death of Nikolenka, the baby son]. . . . God's will shall be done. Since I had no rendezvous on that day, Sergei was not able to notice my state of mind. It was for the first time of the entire past that I was happy not to be with him, for we only would have embarrassed each other. Dear Maman, when will you give me a positive reply concerning the favor which I have asked you already a year ago? I entrust you my fate; obtain this single favor that will assure me peace on this earth: get me a permit to be confined with Sergei and I will forget all my sorrows . . . .

Your subservient daughter
Marie Volkonskaya[11]

---

[11] *Russkie propilei,* I, 60.

K

Reminiscences from the Memoirs of P. Y. Annenkova

On March 16, 1829, there was born my daughter, whom we named in honor of her grandmother, Anna. Alexandra Grigorevna Muravieva gave birth to Nonushka, and Davydova to a boy, Vaka. We were amused when the old fellow, our Commandant [Leparsky], discovered that we were pregnant; he found it out from our letters which he is obliged to read. We wrote to our relatives, asking them to send us clothes for our expected babies. The old fellow returned to us our letters and came to explain:

"Look, permit me to say, that you have no right to be pregnant," he stated haltingly, in great confusion. "When the births begin, well, then it is another matter."

I do not know why it seemed to him that after the babies were born everything became legal, but not before.

Upon his return to Moscow, an officer was asked to deliver a letter from Pauline to her mother-in-law, for which he was paid 100 rubles by Anna Ivanovna Annenkova. Being more honest than wise, he declared to his superior officer, that he brought a letter from the wife of a state criminal for which he was paid one hundred rubles. The episode was reported to Nicholas I and when Leparsky was told about it, he called in Pauline Annenkova, greatly agitated. The following account is cited by Pauline:

"The Commandant sent for me and when I appeared, he received me in an unusual manner, locking the door behind me. I laughed and asked him, why such caution. When, however, I learned about the cause of all this, I did not laugh any more. Leparsky began to ask me: 'Did you write a letter, Madame?' I wrote only one letter, I replied. Leparsky kept asking me specifically, what I had written in the letter that unexpectedly reached Nicholas I. Then I said that 'I only wrote, Monsieur General, that you are an honest man, and that packages be sent in your care and not to Irkutsk where they might be lost." The old man grabbed his head in both hands, and pacing the floor, he kept saying: 'I am lost!' Sometimes Leparsky was very amusing, but what a wonderful man he was!"[12]

[12] P. Y. Annenkova, *Zapiski zheny dekabrista* (Petrograd, Knigoizdatel'stvo 'Prometei', n.d.), 136-137; 138-139. New ed. 182 ff.

L

Concerning Installation of
Windows for the Decembrists

December 6, 1830
St. Petersburg

Dear Madame, Princess Elizaveta Alexandrovna!

I hereby transmit the letter of Marie Nikolayevna Volkonskaya to Your Excellency, from the Petrovsky prison. I consider it my duty to inform you, Dear Madame, that his Imperial Highness, having received from the Commandant, General Leparsky, a report on the building of this prison, on his own accord and for reasons of boundless magnanimity, deigned to order that clear windows be installed, etc.

At the same time, I am unable not to mention, that wives who share the fate of their unfortunate husbands of their own choice in the same prison, by their excessive complaints against accidental though unavoidable errors show ingratitude toward monarchical compassion. [The Emperor] had already done everything possible to alleviate the lot of the prisoners, and repealed for their comfort some of the regulations and fundamental ordinances.

Respectfully and loyally,
I have the honor to be,
Your Excellency, Your
Obedient Servant,
A. Benckendorff[13]

[13] *Letopisi. Dekabristy* (Moscow, 1938), book III, 21.

M

The Case of Charles P. Mazer, the Painter Who Was Forbidden to Paint the Wife of A. M. Muravieva

Tobolsk Deputy Chief of Police
December 15, 1850

To His Excellency, the Civil
Governor of Tobolsk

I have the honor to report to Your Excellency that recently there arrived in Tobolsk a foreigner, some sort of a painter they say, to draw portraits. He did not present his passport to the police and therefore I issued a strict order to Petukhov, Sheriff of the Second District, that from this date on, he make a search and present the results to the police.

The reason for not registering his passport with the police presumably is as follows, I discovered underhandedly: The person hiding from the police is the painter who is making a portrait of the wife of the state criminal Muraviev; she visited the painter at his home yesterday and today.

Since according to rule No. 135 of 1845 state and political criminals as exiled persons are strictly forbidden from having their portraits painted, and we have evidence to this effect, I have the honor, Your Excellency, to request clarification: Does this rule apply to the wives [of the Decembrists]? If it does, then what measures must I undertake presently? It is particularly important since, presumably under the pretense of painting their wives, they may also make portraits of the men. In any case, Muravieva has asked on her own for preliminary permission.

Be that as it may, Muravieva cannot deny that she is being painted nor when he is found can the painter, who will also confirm that he is painting her portrait. Besides, we have other evidence. However, I do not dare to drop in suddenly at the home of Muravieva, to investigate on the spot, without the permission of Your Excellency. As you yourself know, Muraviev in his luxurious way of life and frequent parties enjoys some influence in society and the reputation of a popular host. I therefore hesitated to adopt police measures for which I may be penalized. Awaiting the permission of Your Excellency, I have the honor to report, that I will continue to investigate the painter and whatever I find I will immediately have the honor to report.

Deputized Chief of Police
Efremov[14]

Additional Report

Ayant commencé un portrait-groupe de Madame Mouravieff et de ses enfant, je l'ai discontinue, parce que Mr. Mouravieff m'a dit que Monsieur le Gouverneru lui avait exprimé le désir, qu'il ne continuât pas ce portrait.

Tobolsk Décembre 1850.   Charles P. Mazer

---

[14] *Letopisi. Dekabristy* (Moscow, 1938), book III, 23.

Biographical Data

ANNENKOV, IVAN ALEKSANDROVICH (1802-1878). Lieutenant of the Horseguard Regiment. Member of the Southern Society. Sentenced to twenty years; reduced to fifteen. Sent to Nerchinsk in 1827. Restored to all rights by the amnesty of 1856. Married Pauline Geueble (1800-1876) in Petrovsk, Siberia.

BASARGIN, NIKOLAI VASILEVICH (1799-1861). Lieutenant. Member of the Southern Society. Sentenced to twenty years, reduced to fifteen and later to ten. In 1827 sent to Nerchinsk. Sent into exile in 1835 to Turinsk (Tobolsk) and a year later to Kurgan. Returned to western Russia in 1856. Left memoirs.

BESTUZHEV, NIKOLAI ALEKSANDROVICH (1791-1855). Naval Lieutenant. Member of the Northern Society. Mason. Sentenced to life imprisonment later reduced to twenty years, to fifteen, and then to thirteen. In 1839 exiled to Seleginsk (Irkutsk). Talented portraitist and writer. Left memoirs.

BORISOV, ANDREI IVANOVICH (1798-1854). Second Lieutenant. Founder of the Society of United Slavs. Sentenced to life imprisonment, reduced to twenty years. Sent to Nerchinsk in 1826. In 1832 sentence reduced to fifteen and in 1835 to thirteen years. Sent into exile in 1839 to Podlopatino (Verkhneudinsk); two years later to Malaya Razvodnaya. Lived with his brother Piotr. Mentally ill. On September 30, 1854, when his brother suddenly died, Andrei Borisov committed suicide.

BORISOV, PIOTR IVANOVICH (1800-1854). Lieutenant. Member of the Society of United Slavs. Sentenced to life imprisonment, reduced to twenty years. Sent to Nerchinsk in 1826. In 1832 sentence reduced to fifteen and in 1835 to thirteen years. Sent in 1839 into exile to Podlopatino (Verkhneudinsk)

123

and two years later to Malaya Razvodnaya. Died in 1854 (*see* Borisov, Andrei). Talented color painter.

DAVYDOV, VASILII L'VOVICH (1792-1855). Colonel. Member of the Southern Society. Sentenced to life imprisonment, reduced to twenty years and sent to Nerchinsk. Sentence reduced to fifteen and in 1845 to thirteen years. In 1839 sent into exile to Krasnoyarsk where he died a year before the general amnesty. Married Alexandra Ivanovna Potapova who followed him to Siberia.

FONVIZIN, MIKHAIL ALEKSANDROVICH (1788-1854). Major-General, retired. Member of the Northern Society. Sentenced to twenty years, reduced to eight. Sent to Nerchinsk in 1828. Exiled to Yenisseisk, in 1835 to Krasnoyarsk and then to Tobolsk. Married Natalia Dmitrievna Apukhtina, who joined her husband in Irkutsk in 1828. All children born in Siberia died at an early age. Two sons left in Russia before exile to Siberia.

IVASHEV, VASILI PETROVICH (1794-1840). Cavalry captain. Member of the Southern Society. Sentenced to twenty years; reduced to fifteen and later to ten. Sent to Nerchinsk in 1827. Exiled in 1835 to Turinsk (Tobolsk). Married Camilla Petrovna Ledantu, French born, in Siberia. She died in 1839 in Turinsk of child birth. Left three children, six, four, and two. Ivashev died exactly one year after Camilla.

LUNIN, MIKHAIL SERGEEVICH (1787-1845). Lieutenant Colonel, member of the Northern Society. Sentenced to twenty years, reduced to fifteen, then to ten. Sent to Nerchinsk in 1828. One of the most outspoken opponents of the government. For his "insolent thoughts and judgment" was sent to one of the most isolated distant prisons at Akatui, where he died in 1845. All pleas of his sister, Countess Uvarova, were turned down. Lunin authored "A View of the Secret Society in Russia" and other essays.

MUKHANOV, PIOTR ALEKSANDROVICH (1799-1854). Captain. Member of the Northern Society. Sentenced to twelve years, reduced to eight. In 1828 sent to Nerchinsk. Exiled in 1832 to Bratsky Ostrog (Irkutsk), later to Ust-Kudinskoe (Irkutsk) and, finally, to Irkutsk.

MURAVIEV, ALEXANDER MIKHAILOVICH (1802-1853). Cornet of the Horseguard regiment. Member of the Northern Society. Sentenced to twelve years, reduced to eight. Sent to Nerchinsk in 1827, to be exiled in 1833, but volunteered to remain in prison, awaiting expiration of term of his brother, Nikita Muraviev. In 1835, Alexander, his brother Nikita, and Dr. F. B. Wolfe were all exiled to the village of Urik (Irkutsk).

MURAVIEV, ARTAMON ZAKHAROVICH (1794-1846). Colonel. Member of the Southern Society. Sentenced to life imprisonment, reduced to twenty, later to fifteen, finally, to thirteen years. Sent to Irkutsk, then to Nerchinsk. Made a living selling meat and fish while in exile. As a result of an accident died after a short illness. All pleas that he be sent as a volunteer private to the Caucasus were turned down by Nicholas I.

MURAVIEV, NIKITA MIKHAILOVICH (1795-1843). Captain of the Guard. Member of the Northern Society. Author of the Constitutional Project. Sentenced to twenty, later reduced to to eighteen, and eventually to ten years. Sent to Nerchinsk in 1827. In 1835, together with his brother Alexander, sent into exile to Urik (Irkutsk), where he died after a short illness. His wife, Countess Alexandra (Alexandrina) Grigorevna, joined him in Siberia in Nerchinsk, where she died in 1832.

NARYSHKIN, MIKHAIL MIKHAILOVICH (1798-1863). Member of the Northern Society. Sentenced to twelve, reduced to eight years. Sent to Nerchinsk in 1827. Exiled in 1832 to Kurgan (Tobolsk). In 1837 was sent to the Caucasus as a volunteer private. Retired in 1844 to reside under strict orders in the village of Vysokoye (Tula) and "nowhere else." Freed from surveillance in 1855. Regained freedom a year later according to the amnesty. Married Countess Elizaveta Petrovna Konovnitsyna, who followed her husband to Siberia. Childless, they adopted a six-month old girl, Ulyana Chupyatova.

OBOLENSKY, YEVGENI PETROVICH (1798-1865). Lieutenant. Member of the Northern Society. Sentenced to life, reduced to twenty, then to fifteen, and finally to thirteen years. Sent to Nerchinsk in 1826. In 1835 exiled to the village of Itantsinskoe (Irkutsk) and then to Turinsk (Tobolsk). In 1842 sent to Yalutorovsk. Returned to Kaluga in 1856. In 1846 married Varvara Samsonovna Baranova, a former serf girl.

ODOEVSKY, ALEXANDER IVANOVICH (1802-1839). Cornet. Member of the Northern Soceity. Sentenced to twelve, later reduced to eight years. In 1832 exiled and placed as a laborer at the Telminsk State Factory, in Irkutsk Province. Later exiled to Yelani (Irkutsk), then to Ishim (Tobolsk) in 1836. In 1837 sent to the Caucasus as a private. Died of malaria in 1839.

POGGIO, IVAN IVANOVICH (1798-1873). Lieutenant-colonel. Member of the Southern Society. Sentenced to life, reduced to twenty, later to fifteen, and finally to thirteen years. Sent to Nerchinsk in 1827. In 1839 exiled to the village of Ust'-Kudinskoye (Irkutsk). Freed in 1856. Married Larisa Andreevna Smirnova in Irkutsk.

PUSHCHIN, IVAN IVANOVICH (1798-1859). Judge. Member of the Northern Society. Sentenced to twenty years. In 1839 was exiled to Turinsk (Tobolsk) and in 1842 to Yalutorovsk. In 1856, according to the amnesty, returned to western Russia. Resided in Petersburg. Married the widow of the Decembrist Fonvizin, Natalia Dmitrievna.

ROSEN, ANDREI YEVGENIEVICH (1800-1884). Lieutenant. Member of the Northern Society. Sentenced to ten years later reduced to six. Sent to Nerchinsk in 1827. In 1832 exiled to Kurgan (Tobolsk). In 1837 sent to the Caucasus as a private. Retired in 1839. Sent to Narva (Estonia) to live with his brother "under strict surveillance." Regained his freedom according to the 1856 amnesty. Left memoirs. Married Anna Vasilievna Malinovskaya who joined her husband in Siberia in 1830. In 1856 the children regained the title of "Baron."

STEINGEL, VLADIMIR IVANOVICH (1783-1862). Lieutenant-Colonel. Member of the Northern Society. Sent to Nerchinsk in 1827. In 1836 exiled to Yelan' (Irkutsk) and later to Ishim

(Tobolsk) in 1837. Returned to Tver in 1856 and two years later was freed from surveillance. Left memoirs. Married the daughter of the Director of the Custom House of Kyakhta, Pelageya Petrovna Vonifatsieva.

SUTGOFF, ALEXANDER NIKOLAYEVICH (1801-1872). Lieutenant. Member of the Northern Society. Sentenced to life, later reduced to twenty, then to fifteen and, finally, to thirteen years. In 1827 sent to Nerchinsk. Exiled to the village of Vvedenskaya (Irkutsk) in 1839. Later transferred to Malaya Razvodnaya. In 1848 sent as a private to the Caucasus.

SVISTUNOV, PIOTR NIKOLAYEVICH (1803-1889). Kornet. Member of the Northern and Southern Societies. Sentenced to twenty, reduced to fifteen and later to ten years. In 1827 sent to Nerchinsk. In 1835 exiled to the village of Idinskoye (Irkutsk) and later to Kurgan. Freed by the amnesty of 1856, though he remained under strict surveillance until 1860.

TRUBETSKOY, SERGEI PETROVICH (1790-1860). Lieutenant-colonel. Member of the Northern Society. Sentenced to life, reduced to twenty, then to fifteen, and finally to thirteen years. Exiled to Oyek (Irkutsk) in 1839. Married Yekaterina (Katasha) Ivanovna Laval (1800-1854), first woman to follow her husband to Siberia. In 1845 Trubetskaya and her children were permitted by special order to live in Irkutsk on account of her poor health. Katasha died in 1854 in Irkutsk. In 1856 Trubetskoy was allowed to return to western Russia. His noble rank was restored to him, though not his title "Prince." Left Memoirs.

VADKOVSKY, FEODOR FEODOROVICH (1800-1844). Lieutenant. Member of the Southern Society. Sentenced to life, then reduced to twenty, again to fifteen, finally, to thirteen years. Sent to Nerchinsk in 1828. In 1839, because of illness, exiled to Oyek (Irkutsk) where he died.

VOLKONSKY, SERGEI GRIGOREVICH (1788-1865). Major-General. Mason. Member of the Northern and Southern Societies. Sentenced to twenty years and reduced in 1832 to ten. Sent to Nerchinsk in 1826. Exiled to the village of Urik (Irkutsk) in 1836. Granted freedom according to the 1856 amnesty. Married Marie Nikolayevna Rayevskaya (1805-1863) in 1825, daughter of General N. N. Rayevsky. Left memoirs. Four children. Marie was the second wife, after Katasha, to follow her husband to Siberia.

WOLFE, FERDINAND BOGDANOVICH (? -1854). Army physician. Member of the Southern Society. Sentenced to twenty years, reduced to fifteen. Sent to Nerchinsk in 1827. Exiled to the village of Urik (Irkutsk). Permitted to practice medicine in exile in 1836.

YAKUBOVICH, ALEXANDER PETROVICH (1792-1845). Captain. Did not belong to any society, though he participated in discussions and supported verbally radical action. Temperamental, favored regicide or, at least, considered it desirable. His militant bitterness at times explained by a severe head injury which frequently caused him agonizing pain. Wore a band around his head all the time. Sentenced to life, reduced to twenty, then to fifteen, and finally, to thirteen years. In 1826 he was sent to Nerchinsk and in 1839 exiled to the village of Bolshoye-Razvodnoye (Irkutsk) and later to Nazimovo (Yeniseisk).

YAKUSHKIN, IVAN DMITRIEVICH (1796-1857). Captain. Member of the Northern Society. Sentenced to twenty years, reduced to fifteen and then to thirteen. In 1827 sent to Nerchinsk. In 1835 exiled to Yalutorovsk. Freed by the amnesty of 1856. Left memoirs. Forbade his wife to join him in Siberia unless she was to bring the children with her. Family remained in western Russia.

YENTAL'TSEV, ANDREI VASILEVICH (1788-1845). Lieutenant-colonel. Member of the Southern Society. Sentenced to two years of hard labor, reduced to one. Sent to Nerchinsk in 1827. Married to Alexandra Vasilevna Lisovskaya who followed her husband in Siberia. Yental'tsev had many difficulties with the administration. Became mentally ill and was found incurable. He died in 1845.

YUSHNEVSKY, ALEXANDER PETROVICH (1786-1844). Member of the Southern Society. Sentenced to twenty years, reduced to fifteen, and later to thirteen. In 1827 was sent to

Nerchinsk. In 1839 exiled to the village of Kuz'minskaya (Irkutsk). Ordered the epitaph on his gravestone to read: "I need nothing." Married Mariya Kazimirovna Krulikovskaya. In 1828 she joined her husband in Siberia.

Select Bibliography

Amfiteatrov, A. *Zhenshchiny v obshchestvennykh dvizheniyakh Rossii.* St. Petersburg, 1907.

Annenkova, P. Y. *Vospominaniya Poliny Annenkovoy.* Moscow, 1932. An earlier edition: *Zapiski zheny dekabrista.* Petrograd, "Prometey," [1915].

Basargin, N. V. *Zapiski.* Petrograd, 1917.

Bestuzheva, K. *Zheny dekabristov.* Moscow, 1913.

Chernov, S. N. "Dekabristy na puti v Blagodatsk," *Katorga i ssylka,* Book XVIII, 1925, 246-275.

Dekabristy na katorge i v ssylke. Moscow, 1926.

Dekabristy v Buryatii. [*Sbornik statei*]. Verkhneudinsk, 1927.

Dekabristy v Zabaikalye. Neizdannye materialy. Ed. by A. V. Kharchevnikov. Chita, 1925.

Frantseva, M. D. "Vospominaniya." *Istorichesky vestnik,* V. 1888, 381-412; VI, 618-640; VII, 61-87.

Gernet, M. N. *Istoriya tsarskoy tyurmy.* 2nd edition. Moscow, Vol. II, pp. 193-208.

Golovachev, P. M. *Dekabristy. Materialy dlya kharakteristiki.* Moscow, 1907.

Golubovsky, P. V. *Pis'ma dekabrista A. P. Yushnevskogo i ego zheny M. K. iz Sibiri.* Kiev, 1908.

Gornfeld, A. " 'Russkie zhenshchiny' Nekrasova v novom osveshchenii," *Russkoye bogatstvo,* IV, 1904, 2-52.

"Imperator Nikolai i semeistvo dekabrista Ivana Aleksandrovicha Annenkova," *Russkaya starina,* III, 1901, 673-678.

"K istorii dekabristov." Reported by A. E. P. *Istorichesky vestnik,* V, 1898, 675-677.

"K istorii dekabristov," *Russkaya starina,* III, 1896, 610.

Khin, M. M. "Zheny dekabristov," *Istorichesky vestnik,* XII, 1884, 650-683.

Kologrivov, [Father] Ivan. "Knyaginya Ekaterina Ivanovna Trubetskaya," *Sovremennye zapiski* (Paris), LX, 1936, 294-249; LXI, 1936, 231-279; LXII, 1936, 247-284.

Kubalov, B. G. "Dekabristy i amnistiya," *Sibirskie ogni,* V, 1924, 143-159.

Kubalov, B. G. *Dekabristy v Irkutske i na blizhaishikh k nemu zavodakh.* Irkutsk, 1925.

Letopisi. Dekabristy. Moscow, Gosudarstvennyi Literaturnyi Muzei. Ed. by N. P. Chulkov. Moscow, 1938.

Maksimov, S. *Sibir i katorga.* St. Petersburg, 1900.

Mazour, Anatole G. *The First Russian Revolution, 1825. The Decembrist Movement, its Origin, Development, and Significance.* Stanford University Press, 1967.

Nekrasov, N. *Russian Women.* Tr. By Juliet M. Soskice. Oxford University Press, 1929.

Okun', S. B. *Dekabrist M. S. Lunin.* Leningrad, 1962.

"Pis'ma M. N. Volkonskoy iz Sibiri, 1827-1831 gg.," *Russkie propilei,* I, 1915, 1-81.

Poggio, A. V. "Zapiski," in *Vospominaniya i rasskazy deyatelei tainykh obshchestv 1820-kh godov* (Moscow, 1931), I, 22-90.

Pokrovsky, V. (Comp.) *Zheny dekabristov. Sbornik istoriko-bytovykh statei.* Moscow, 1906.

"Provody knyagini Marii Volkonskoy, 1826 g. [v Sibir]," *Russkaya starina,* IV, 1875, 822-827.

Reiser, S. "Nekrasov v rabote nad 'Russkimi zhenshchinami'," *Zvenya,* VI, 1936, 701-736.

Rosen, A. S. *Zapiski dekabrista.* St. Petersburg, 1907.

Shchegolev, P. E. "Zheny dekabristov i vopros ob ikh yuridicheskikh pravakh," in *Istoricheskie etyudy,* (St. Petersburg, 1913), 395-441.

Shchegolev, P. E. "Podvig russkoi zhenshchiny," *Istorichesky vestnik,* V, 1904, 530-550.

Shenrok, V. "Odna iz zhen dekabristov," *Russkoye bogatstvo,* XI, 1894, 100-136; XII, 54-92.

Steingel, V. I. "Zapiski," *Obshchestvennye dvizheniya v Rossii,* I, 321-475.

Storozhenko, N. V. "K istorii dekabristov," *Istorichesky vestnik,* I, 1894, 272-274.

Trubetskoy, S. P. *Zapiski.* Ed. by his daughter. St. Petersburg, 1907.

Venturi, Franco. *Il moto decabrista ei i fratelli Poggio.* Milan, G. Einaudi, 1956.

Venevitinov, M. A. "Roman dekabrista [V. P. Ivasheva]." *Russkaya mysl',* X, 1885, 116-142.

Veresov, L. *Podvig russkoy zhenshchiny.* [M. N. Volkonskaya]. St. Petersburg, 1906.

Volkonskaya, Marie Nikolayevna. "Rasskazy iz proshlogo." Reported by T. Novosiltseva, in *Russkaya starina,* VI, 1878, 336-342.

Volkonskaya, Marie Nikolayevna. *Zapiski.* St. Petersburg, 1906.

Volkonskaya, Marie Nikolayevna. *Zapiski.* Tr. from the French. Petrograd, 1916.

Volkonsky, S. G. *Zapiski dekabrista.* St. Petersburg, 1902.

Yakushkin, I. *Zapiski.* Moscow, 1925.

Yakushkin, I. D. *Zapiski, stati, pis'ma dekabrista I. D. Yakushkina.* Moscow, 1951.

Index

Alexander I, 18

Alexander II, 6

Alexander Nikolayevich (Manifesto of 1842), 47

Alexandrovsk, Distillery of, 24

Alexandrovsk silver melting plants, 2

Amnesty, 53, 76, 90

Annenkov, Ivan A., 85, 86-87, 92

Annenkova, Praskovya Yegorovna (Pauline), 7, 9, 10, 85f, 86, 87, 88, 89, 90, 91, 92, 110, 113, 117.

Atkinson, Thomas W., 52f.

Bagration, P. I. Prince, 39

Barsukov, N., 95f.

Basargin, N. V., 43

Bastille, Fall of, 36

Belyayev, A. P., 95

Benkendorff, Count A., 71f., 120

Blagodatsk, Mines of, 25

Borisov brothers (Peter and Andrey), 2, 29, 52

Breshkovskaya, Catherine, 95

Bulanova, O. K., 84f.

Burnashev, T., 89

Charles I (France), 36

Charpantié, Mme., 86

Chernyshev, A. P., 39

Chita, Prison of, 25, 30, 35

Damskaya ulitsa, see Ladies Street

Davydov, A. V., 54

Davydov, V. L., 2f., 29, 39, 47, 54

Davydova, A. I., 5, 35, 88, 110

Decembrism and Nicholas I, 23

Dibich, Count I. I., 113

Dinocours, 80

Dolgorukov, Prince, 6

Elena Pavlovna, Grand Duchess, 16

Figner, Vera, 95

Fonvizina, N. D., 5, 9, 99, 110

Fonvizins, 40

Gernet, M. N., 95f.

Geueble, Pauline, see Annenkova Praskovya Yegorovna

Grigorovich, V., 80

Ivashev, Vasily, 43, 79, 85

Ivasheva, Camilla, 9, 80-81, 84

Katasha, see Trubetskaya

Katorzhniki, see poselentsy, 33f.

Kennan, George, 33f.

Khin, M. M., 95f.

Kitushka (Muraviev), 46

Konovnitsyn, Count P., 92

Kozitskaya, Alexandra G. (Kozitsky family), 13, 16

Kubalov, B. G., 53f.

Kuz'mina, Mlle (Governess), 45, 49

"Ladies Club", 84

"Ladies Street," see Damskaya ulitsa, 37

Lanskoy, V. Ya., 86

Laval, also Jean Charles François de Laval de la Loubrerie, 13, 16, 18, 19, 20, 21, 42, 45, 49-50

Lavinsky, A. S., Governor-General, 3, 4, 10, 99, 113.

Lebzeltern, Count Gustav, 19

Ledantu, Mme, 80

Ledantu, Camilla P., see Ivasheva

Leparsky, S. R. (Commandant), 36, 37, 71, 84, 90, 114

Lomonosov, M. V., 60

Lunin, M. S., 30, 41

Mazer, Charles P., 121, 122

Maksimov, Ivan, 103

Manifesto of 1839, 42

Marx, Karl, 56

Matveev, A., 113

Mazour, Anatole G., 2f., 60f.

Mirsky, Prince D. S., 11f., 79f.

Mukhanov, P. A., 52

Muraviev, A. M., 121

Muraviev, Artamon, 2f., 29, 48
Muraviev, N. N., see Muraviev-Amursky
Muraviev, Nikita (son of Sergei M.), 42.
Muraviev-Amursky, N. N., 57, 75
Muravieva, Alexandra G. (Alexandrina), 27, 35, 39, 40, 71, 88, 110
"My December Friends", 95
Naryshkina, Elizabeth P., 9, 51, 92, 106, 110
Naryshkins, 40
Nekrasov, N. A. (poet), 8, 11, 79
Nerchinsk, 25, 35
Nesselrode, Count K. V., 89
Nicholas I, 7, 9, 10, 23, 29, 33f, 49, 65, 88, 95
Nikolayevsky, Salt Mines of, 24
Novikov, S., 113
Obolensky, Yevgeny P., 29, 67, 84
Odoyevsky, A. I., 8, 41
Orlov, M. F., 60
Oyek, Village of, 44, 45, 46, 74
Paul I, 13
Pauline, see Annenkova
Perovskaya, Sophia, 95
Pestel, P. I., 80, 81
Petrovsk, Petrovsky zavod, Petrovsky Prison, Petrovsky ostrog, 2, 33, 35, 40, 70, 119
Poggio, A. V., 52, 73
Pokrovsky, V., 3f., 11f., 101f.
Popova, O., 70f., 73f.
Poselentsy, see also katorzhniki, 33f.
Potapov family, 39
Pushchin, I. I., 40, 84
Pushkin, A. S., vi, 41-42, 60, 61
Rayevsky, General N. N., vi, 57, 62, 63, 69
Rayevsky, Nikolai, 60
Repnin, N. G., 108f.
Repnina, Princess, 113
Rosen, Baron A., 17, 61, 93
Rosen, Baroness Anna V., 5, 8, 88, 93
Rupert, Governor V. Ya., 48, 49, 75
Sancy, Mme., 80-81
Shakhovskoi, E. A., 71f.
Shchegolev, P. E., 4f., 57

Shtraikh, Ya., 73f.
Steingel, V. I., 41
Svistunov, P. N., 43
Trubetskaya, Alexandra, 55
Trubetskaya, Yekaterina (Katasha), 5, 8, 9, 10, 13, 21, 26, 27, 29, 33, 35, 40, 42, 43, 44, 45, 49, 50, 52, 53, 66, 88, 92, 104. Children: Liza, 55; Sashenka, 31-32; Sonya, 47, 52; Vanya, 44.
Trubetskaya, Zinaida, 55
Trubetskoy, Prince Sergei, 2, 9, 17, 18, 24, 29, 30, 31, 37, 41, 42, 44, 45, 48, 51, 52, 54, 55, 56, 67
Trubetskoy, Vladimir, 44
Urik, Village of, 72
Usolsk, Salt mines of, 24
Uvarov, Count S. S., 95
Vadkovsky, A. F., 39, 45
Vaucher, Charles, 21
Venturi, Franco, 73f.
Volkonskaya, Elena, 76
Volkonskaya, Princess Marie, 6, 8, 9, 29, 30, 57, 60, 61, 67, 69, 70, 74, 75, 88, 102, 106, 108, 111, 115, 116, 119
Volkonsky, Mikhail (son of Sergei), 75
Volkonsky, Nikolenka, 61, 62, 69
Volkonsky, Prince Peter M., 18, 43, 48
Volkonsky, Prince Sergei, 2f., 19, 24, 27f., 50, 52, 55, 61, 62, 72
Voronki, Estate of, 76-77
Wolfe, Dr. F. B., 43, 72, 73
Yakubovich, A., 2f.
Yakushkin, I. D., 4, 5f, 7f, 29, 65
Yakushkina, Mme, 4, 5f, 7f, 65
Yazykova, 80
Yental'tsev, A. V., 93
Yental'tseva, Mme V. G., 6, 9, 106, 107
Yushnevskaya, Mme, 5, 6
Yushnevsky, A. P., 6, 41
Zavalishin, D. I., 73
Zeidler, Governor I. B., 3, 11, 25, 26, 66, 99, 104
Zhukovsky, V. A., 60, 92
Zinaida, Countess (wife of Count Gustav Lebzeltern, sister of Katasha), 19, 30, 32, 33, 42, 45, 47, 48, 52, 111

BOOKS FROM THE DIPLOMATIC PRESS, INC.

1102 BETTON ROAD, TALLAHASSEE, FLORIDA 32303, U.S.A.

Satow, Sir Ernest. *Korea and Manchuria between Russia and Japan 1895–1904. The Observations of Sir Ernest Satow, British Minister and Plenipotentiary to Japan and China.* Selected and edited with a historical introduction by George Alexander Lensen. First published 1966; second printing 1968. 300 pp., collotype frontispiece. cloth. ISBN 0-910512-01-9. $12.50.
". . . a welcome addition to primary source material for the study of Far Eastern diplomatic history." — *The Journal of Asian Studies*
". . . full of interesting and illuminating views from a diplomat of experience and wisdom. . ." — *The American Historical Review*

D'Anethan, Baron Albert. *The d'Anethan Dispatches from Japan 1894–1910. The Observations of Baron Albert d'Anethan, Belgian Minister Plenipotentiary and Dean of the Diplomatic Corps.* Translated and edited with a historical introduction by George Alexander Lensen. 1967. 272 pp., collotype frontispiece. cloth. ISBN 0-910512-02-7. $15.00.
"A companion volume to . . . Sir Ernest Satow . . . Masterfully selected excerpts of heretofore unpublished official dispatches . . ." — *Historische Zeitschrift*
"Valuable to students in East Asian international relations." — *Choice*

Lensen, George Alexander. *The Russo-Chinese War.* 1967. 315 pp., collotype frontispiece, maps, extensive bibliography. cloth. ISBN O-910512-03-05. $15.00.
"The first full-length treatment of Sino-Russian hostilities in Manchuria during the Boxer Rebellion of 1900 . . . Lensen writes clearly, vividly, and with full mastery of his subject." — *Choice*

Will, John Baxter. *Trading Under Sail off Japan 1860–1899.* The Recollections of Captain John Baxter Will, Sailing-Master and Pilot. Edited with a historical introduction by George Alexander Lensen. 1968. 190 pp., lavishly printed and illustrated, cloth. ISBN 0-910512-04-3./ $12.50.
". . . this extremely interesting story . . . ranks with the few which, while not perhaps of the type to keep young children from play, should keep most men 'in the chimney corner.' " — *The Japan Times*

Lensen, George Alexander (comp.). *Japanese Diplomatic and Consular Officials in Russia. A Handbook of Japanese Representatives in Russia from 1874 to 1968.* 1968. 230 pp., hardcover. ISBN 0-910512-05-1. $15.00.
"A useful handbook for every serious student of the relations between Japan and the U.S.S.R." — *Narody Azii i Afriki*

Lensen, George Alexander (comp.). *Russian Diplomatic and Consular Officials in East Asia. A Handbook of the Representatives of Tsarist Russia and the Provisional Government in China, Japan and Korea from 1858 to 1924 and of Soviet Representatives in Japan from 1925 to 1968.* 1968. 294 pp., hardcover. ISBN 0-910512-06-X. $15.00
"The two handbooks are essential reference works for every library of East Asian or Russian history: for specialists in the field of Russian-East Asian relations where the author is known as a distinguished pioneering scholar, they will be indispensable companions." — *Pacific Affairs*

Lensen, George Alexander. *Faces of Japan: A Photographic Study.* 154 large collotype reproductions, beautifully printed in a limited edition. 1968. 312 pp., cloth. ISBN 0-910512-07-8. $25.00 (originally $30.00).
Japanese of all walks of life at work and at play, as seen through they eyes of a historian.
"A terrifically beautiful book." — *Wilson Hicks*

Westwood, J. N. *Witnesses of Tsushima.* 1970. xiv, 321 pp. plus 38 illustrations, cloth. ISBN 0-910512-08-06. $15.00.
"Dr. Westwood by interweaving his own narrative with eyewitness accounts and the official reports both Russian and Japanese gives us a far more accurate version of the famous Russian voyage out of Kronstadt to the Straits of Tsushima and the subsequent battle than has been available heretofore." — *Journal of Asian Studies*

Lensen, George Alexander. *Japanese Recognition of the U.S.S.R.: Soviet-Japanese Relations 1921 — 1930.* 1970. viii, 425 pp. illustrated. cloth. ISBN 0-910512-09-4. $15.00.
"This book is a careful detailed treatment of an important period in Russo-Japanese relations. It will be of special interest to diplomatic and economic historians and of more general interest to those concerned with Japan's position in East Asia or the Soviet Union's relations there." — *Choice*

Lensen, George Alexander. *April in Russia: A Photographic Study.* 100 large collotype reproductions, beautifully printed in a limited edition. 1970. 208 pp., cloth. ISBN 0-910512-10-8. $30.00 (originally $40.00).
A historian's view of daily life in the U.S.S.R.
"An enlightening education tool as well as an artistic, almost poetic, addition to personal libraries." — *Tallahassee Democrat*
". . . this historian has the soul of a poet and the eye of an artist." — *Novoye Russkoye Slovo*

McNally, Raymond T. *Chaadayev and his Friends. An Intellectual History of Peter Chaadayev and his Russian Contemporaries.* 1971. vi, 315 pp., frontispiece, imitation leather. ISBN 0-910512-11-6. $15.00.
A new and highly readable interpretation of the place of Peter Chaadayev (1794 — 1856), the first Russian Westernizer and a unique thinker, in intellectual history, based on research in Soviet archives.

Poutiatine, Countess Olga. *War and Revolution. Excerpts from the Letters and Diaries of the Countess Olga Pontiatine.* Translated and edited by George Alexander Lensen. 1971. vi, 111 pp., illustrated, cloth. ISBN 0-910512-12-4. $12.50.
A moving eyewitness account of the Russian Revolution and of conditions in Russian and Anglo-Russian military hospitals during the First Wold War by the granddaughter of the Russian admiral who competed with Commodore Perry in the opening of Japan.

Sansom, Lady Katherine. *Sir George Sansom and Japan*. A memoir of Sir George Sansom, G. B. E., K. C. M. G., Diplomat Historian, by his wife. 1972. 183 pp., illustrated, cloth. ISBN 0-910512-13-2. $15.00.

The diplomatic and scholarly life of Sir George Sansom, the foremost Western authority on Japan, mirrored in the letters and diary entries of his wife and himself, with unforgettable thumbnail sketches of leading diplomatic, political, military and literary figures in Japan from 1928—1950.

Kutakov, Leonid N. *Japanese Foreign Policy on the Eve of the Pacific War. A Soviet View*. 1972. xiii, 241 pp., frontispiece, cloth. ISBN 9105012-15-0. $15.00.

". . . a tightly knit interpretation of an epochal aspect of modern history (particularly the long essay on Japanese-Russian relations) which will intrigue students of the background of World War II."—*Library Journal*

"Of special interest to students of East Asian international relations and to diplomatic historians generally."—*Choice*

Lensen, George Alexander. *The Strange Neutrality: Soviet-Japanese Relations During the Second World War, 1941—1945*. 1972. xii, 335 pp., illustrated, cloth. ISBN 910512-14-0. $15.00.

"A dispassionate and authoritative account which has a place in every collection on the history of World War II in Asia and the Pacific."—*Library Journal*

". . . written with cogency, balance, and depth."—*History*

"A first rate historical work."—*Choice*

Vishwanathan, Savitri. *Normalization of Japanese-Soviet Relations 1945—1970.* 1973. xii, 190 pp. illustrated, cloth. ISBN 910512-14-0. $15.00.

An examination of the political, economic and diplomatic relations between Japan and the U.S.S.R. since the Pacific War, with chapters on trade, fisheries, and the territorial dispute. Written by an Indian scholar on the basis primarily of Japanese sources.

Lensen, George Alexander. *The Damned Inheritance: The Soviet Union and the Manchurian Crises, 1924—1935*. 1974. xiv, 533 pp., illustrated, cloth. ISBN 910512-17-5. $19.80.

An account of the triangular Russo-Chinese-Japanese struggle over Manchuria and the Chinese Eastern Railway and of American and British reaction thereto, written on the basis of Soviet, Japanese, and British documents.

Mazour, Anatole G. *Women in Exile: Wives of the Decembrists*. 1975. About 160 pp., illustrated, cloth, ISBN 910512-19-1. $15.00.

The dramatic story of the wives and fincées of Russia's first revolutionaries, who following the abortive Decembrist revolt of 1825 chose to follow their men into exile in Siberia.

Flanagan, Scott C. *Pathologies of Decision-Making in Prewar Japan*. 1975. About 128 pp., illustrated, cloth, ISBN 910512-18-3. $15.00.

A lucid analysis of the causes and symptoms of four types of chronic malfunctions that infected the Japanese decision-making process, particularly in the foreign policy area, during the years 1930—1945.